LEMNIAN EARTH
AND
THE EARTHS OF THE AEGEAN

The *Early Materials and Practices Series*
is a series of academic guide books devoted to the archaeology, and to the environmental, industrial and social history of a particular material and the practice(s) associated with it, in a given locality, in the past. The purpose of the series is to revive individual physical landscapes where there is normally little to see in terms of sites and monuments but where nevertheless particular events and processes took place. These events may be retained in the oral traditions or written accounts of the local population but are often little known. The series aims to demonstrate the relevance of these materials and their usually fragile landscapes to the modern world, not simply as places to visit but also as places for further enquiry and possible development based on current and up to date research. *Lemnian Earth and the earths of the Aegean* is the first volume in this series.

The books, which are essentially guidebooks for sites 'off the beaten track', are illustrated with a large number of colour photographs and detailed maps, in a clear and informative style. When appropriate, they are followed by a glossary of terms. The books in the series ' *Early Materials and Practices*' contain both original research as well as results already published in the academic literature, the latter being made available for the first time, to the interested public at large. Potingair Press guarantees that all books in the series are peer reviewed prior to publication.

The logo of Potingair Press is Master Brun (Brown), a potingair (apothecary in Scots), a historical person who lived and practised in Stirling, Scotland, in the late 15th century. His image is depicted in the 17th century Erskine Manuscript. Master Brun and his contemporaries experimented with alchemy but were also dispensers of medicines. Little is known of him outside his practice, but Master Brun, clutching his alembic and looking around him inquisitively, epitomises Scotland's traditional emphasis on education, training and good practice, and with determination to disseminate the benefits received.

EARLY MATERIALS AND PRACTICES SERIES

Reviewers' Comments

"The book successfully brings the 'composition and property of materials' closer to the vast and largely unquantifiable 'universe' of beliefs about health and well-being. It has a substantial academic content and provides access for a non-specialist to little known area of research. Its cross-disciplinarity is fascinating: it demonstrates that such an approach can result in new knowledge. It is a pleasure to read"

Professor Marek Dominiczak,
Clinical Biochemistry and Medical Humanities,
University of Glasgow

"This important book tackles a fascinating historical and scientific issue by relating ancient textual evidence for medical and other uses of mineral materials with chemical and geological realities established by the authors' fieldwork and research. Homer and the ancient Greek dramatists and their uses of myth and legend, and early factual reporters like Galen and Pliny and their evidential practices are related with ancient and modern scientific evidence in a book which is equally open to the archaeologist, the earth-scientist and the classical scholar alike"

Professor Elizabeth Moignard, FSA
Classics, University of Glasgow

"This is a clearly written and well explained important text on a fascinating topic, appropriately illustrated with pictures, maps and diagrams that could form a separate guidebook"

Dr. W.D. Ian Rolfe, FRSE
Palaeontologist and Natural Historian.

First published 2011

Potingair Press
7 Belgrave Terrace
Glasgow, UK

Cover design and Typesettting by Potingair Press
Digitally printed and bound in Great Britain
by Printondemand-worldwide, Peterborough

ISBN   978-0-9568240-0-4

Lemnian Earth
and
the earths of the Aegean

an archaeological guide to
medicines, pigments and washing powders

Effie Photos-Jones   *and*   Allan J Hall

Potingair Press
Glasgow

"perhaps the negative results derived from my analyses are one more proof of the risks posed by the application of chemistry on myths, particularly those that are among the oldest or the most vivid".

Louis De Launay (1895, 16), geologist, on his inability, following detailed chemical analysis, to show what made Lemnian Earth an effective medicine.

Detail from Belon's 16ᵗʰ century map (1588) showing the chapel of Sotira and a pannier in the vicinity of the locality of extraction of Lemnian Earth.

Preface

This book is a rather unconventional archaeological guide in that it does not guide the reader around a museum, a monument or an archaeological site, but rather towards an intangible artefact, like a medicine tablet or a washing powder or a specific pigment for an artist's palette. This intangible artefact is of course part of a physical landscape, so in that respect the book is about both unconventional archaeological artefacts and their landscapes.

Our material world and by extension our material heritage is very much defined by objects and materials that are tangible; we can see and touch their remains, whether exhibited in museums or scattered in the soil. But what about materials that we *know* existed and yet their recovery from within archaeological deposits is so rare that we need to take the relevant writings of the ancient authors at face value?

Plant-based medicines formed the backbone of both ancient and modern pharmacopoeias. The plants have grown wild, or were cultivated because knowledge of their therapeutic properties existed within every culture. But plants and the fields where they grew make precarious archaeological sites. By contrast, minerals and the places of their extractions can be better defined. This is because mining and enrichment processes and associated tools were developed as an empirical understanding of the properties of rocks and minerals developed in relation to the usage they could be put to. We know a lot about ancient marble, flint or obsidian quarries, as we do about potters' clay sources or metal smiths' ore deposits. But the minerals that made up medicines and pigments and cleaning agents have consistently eluded us because they blend so well into their surroundings that they become almost invisible.

This book focuses on the earths, white or off-white clay-based substances, of one geographical region, namely the Aegean. Many ancient authors, amongst them antiquity's most prominent doctors like Galen and Dioscorides, commented on them and their effect on human health, but interestingly chose to describe them not simply as medicines but also as pigments, washing powders or simply potters' clays. We can only infer that different grades served different applications. For artists, preoccupied with colour, it was a matter of great importance to acquire the pigment with the best colour intensity and covering power. Not many people took much notice of what fullers thought best for their trade, being so near the bottom of the social hierarchy, but others spoke on their behalf. Aristophanes tells us in no uncertain terms which washing powder Athenians (and their ladies) thought best to use in the house or the public baths.

The book sets out to address many topics from different fields of study: myths and documentary sources from classical antiquity, geology and pharmacology. It follows the list of earths first compiled by Discorides (see Table 1) and tackles the most prominent ones based on their principal application, namely as medicines, pigments or cleaning agents. But there are others as well, like alum and sulphur, earths, but not in name, in the breadth of their applications. The book presents an overview of the information about the nature of the earths and their properties and applications, provided by the ancient sources as well as later writers and travellers, from the Renaissance to the 19th century.

Very thorough compilations of the literature have already been provided by a number of researchers, so our attention has turned to the islands that gave the earths their names. Based on field work, we present the geological and geochemical background to each island, underpinning the formation of these earths and a description of the likely localities of their extraction; also a guide on how to get to the places by taking in the physical landscape that surrounds the places of their extraction. Geoarchaeological work helps identify localities of extraction of the raw materials, within each island; but are the raw materials, ie the extracted clays, the same materials as the actual artefacts, the medicines or pigments? Is there any current pharmacological research that suggests how the earth, the medicine, may have worked?

We will argue that earths are more than the sum of their parts since they are both composite materials (ie they consist of both clay and other minerals) as well as the result of natural enrichment and humanly engineered beneficiation. Furthermore as substances taken internally, their effectiveness depends on an understanding of how the body reacts to them. Elucidating the nature and conditions of their extraction, processing and packaging and pointing to the biomedical mechanisms by which they may have worked effectively within the body, may have an advantage beyond the obvious one, namely, that of enhancing our understanding of the past. It may shed light on well-established but 'strange' habits displayed by both humans and animals, namely *geophagia*, the intentional consumption of clays. In this book we suggest that the medicinal and other earths of the Aegean, far from being 'dead' and forever relegated to the documentary record of antiquity, are 'alive and well' in their respective islands and 'open' to further investigation and constructive and meaningful development, both by local interested parties as well as the scientific world at large.

Acknowledgements

The authors are grateful to a number of individuals and institutions for their assistance and positive contribution to the research into earths and their importance in antiquity. Our warmest thanks are extended to our co-researchers from, the Institute of Geology and Mineral Exploration (IGME), Athens, Vassilis Perdikatsis, Stathis Chiotis and Eleni Demou for many fruitful discussions and exchange of ideas and data regarding Lemnos and Samos; the technical staff at the Department of Earth Sciences, Glasgow University, Dugie Turner and Murdoch Macleod, William Higginson and Robert McDonald for sample preparation, XRD and SEM analyses. Arbory McNulty (née Cottier) for her expert fieldwork and Michael Malamos for his contribution to bibliography and historical review; Paul Skett and Duncan E. Stewart-Tull of the Department of Life Sciences Glasgow University for their biomedical work; the Director, David Blackman, the Librarian Penny Wilson-Zarganis and the staff at the British School at Athens; Alan Hart and Gordon Cressey of the Natural History Museum, London. The editor of the series Richard Jones and our referees and reviewers for their patience in going through earlier and final versions of the book and their many insightful comments and suggestions, some resulting in major rewrites.

The work on Lemnos and Samos benefitted from joint support in 1998 by the British Council and the Greek General Secretariat of Research and Technology, Greek Ministry of Development, while the work on Melos carried out over a number of years was generously funded by several organisations. This latter work, part of the greater survey of SE Melos, to which many institutions have contributed, has its own forthcoming publication; to those individuals and organizations grateful acknowledgements are offered. Finally, to our respective spouses and families we extend our deep gratitude for persevering with what to them must have undoubtedly seemed an 'unnecessarily' long gestation period for a book on a single topic and a material that 'does not exist'.

Effie Photos-Jones and Allan J Hall
Summer 2011
Glasgow, Scotland

Contents

Galen's query   3

Medicines from plants, minerals and earths   9

Herb-based medicines   9

Clays and Geophagia   12

Earths   17

Lemnian Earth: related myths   22

Lemnian Earth: facts   28

Lemnian Earth: where to find it   32

Kotsinas and Phtheleidia Spring: Belon's route   33

Hephaistias and Kastro Vouni: Galen's route   41

Geological background to Lemnos   50

Alum and astringency   55

Samian Earth   57

Boron   62

Eretrian Earth   64

Cleigenis' Soap   66

Kimolian Earth   68

Chian Earth   70

Apelles' Palette   71

The colour red: Miltos of Kea   73

The colour white: The white rock of Melos   78

The white earth of Melos: Melian Earth   81

Earths but not in name: Melian alum and sulphur   84

Minor earths   88

Belon's scepticism   90

Mineral enrichment as ritual   90

Belon's scepticism addressed?   96

A recipe for Lemnian Earth   96

Concluding Remarks   104

References   106

Glossary   115

Indices   120

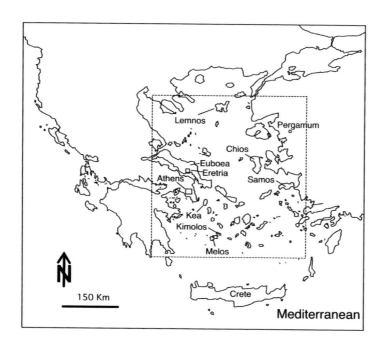

Fig. 1a *Map of Greece with islands and geographical areas mentioned in the text. Boxed area highlighting the greater geographical region discussed in this book.*

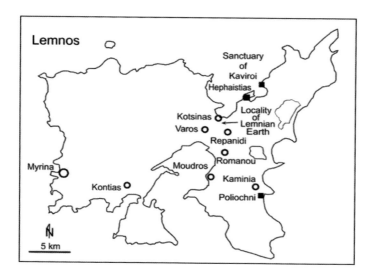

Fig. 1b *Lemnos island showing key places mentioned in this book.*

Galen's query

In the spring of AD 167, Galen, renowned doctor and personal physician to a succession of Roman emperors, set off from Pergamum, his native city on the coast of Asia Minor, via Lemnos (Fig. 1a) in the north-east Aegean, to return to Rome. He had been summoned back by the two emperors, Marcus Aurelius and Lucius Verus, who were spending the winter in the northern Adriatic on account of the outbreak of a plague. However rather than stopping at Hephaistias, in the north of the island (Figs. 1b and 2), the captain put anchor at Myrina bay (Figs. 1b and 3), in the west. Galen was not amused:

"...at first I did not know that there were two towns on the island, but imagined that, as in the case of Samos, Chios ..... and all the other Aegean islands, so also Lemnos would have one single town with the same name as the whole island. But when I landed on the island, I found that the town was called Myrina and that neither the temple of Philoctetes nor the sacred hill of Hephaistos were in the territory of this town, but in the other town, called Hephaisteias which was not near Myrina. Further, the captain was unable to wait" (Galen *On Simple Drugs* IX.II.247-8; trans. Brock 1929, 193).

Galen had to wait for a few years before he could return to Lemnos, this time approaching the island from the north and making certain that he would be dropped off at Hephaistias. He was persistent in his enquiries:

"I also sailed to Lemnos, and for no other reason (as the gods know) than to get the Lemnian earth or 'seal' whichever it is called" (Galen *On Simple Drugs* IX.II.247-8. trans. Brock 1929, 193).

Galen was eager to expand his knowledge of medicinal herbs and minerals, based primarily on Dioscorides' *opus* of medical substances (*De Materia Medica*), and in some respects envied his predecessor's ready access to a wealth of natural materials:

"now Dioscorides and others have given a true description of all the finest drugs that grow in each country, while we, as I say, have to prepare them in the way stated, especially if we live in Rome, where enormous quantities arrive every year from all nations" (Galen *On Simple Drugs* IX.II.247-8; trans. Brock 1929, 198).

Dioscorides, an army doctor in the reign of Nero about one hundred years earlier, had mentioned that Lemnian Earth or Lemnian *miltos* was mixed with goat's blood and that was the reason why it had a red, but unstaining colour. Furthermore, he thought of Lemnian Earth as a valuable antidote to snake bites, which he prescribed as a cure for ulcers and even as a preventive against the plague; all of these reasons were sufficient incentive for Galen to return to Lemnos. If convinced, his plan was to bring back to Rome small *sphragides*, or pellets, for his illustrious clients. But Galen was sceptical about the goat's blood:

"I thought well to inquire whether there was no tradition of goat's blood being mixed with the Earth. All who heard this question of mine laughed, and they were not mere chance individuals, but people well informed about the whole history of the locality as well as in other matters. In fact I got a book from one of them, written by a former native, in which all the uses of the Lemnian Earth were set forth....The man who gave me the book, and who was counted among the leading citizens of Hephaistias, used the medicine himself for many purposes, ...for old standing wounds that were slow to heal, for viper bites and animal bites in general; he also used the seal for poisons, both for prevention and cure. He said that he had also tried a juniper preparation to which some earth is added" (Galen *On Simple Drugs* IX.II.247-8; trans. Brock 1929, 194).

Fig. 2 *Entrance to the port of Hephaistias seen in the far distance and viewed looking south from the cliffs above the sanctuary of Kaveiroi (Kaveirion). Galen would have sailed into that bay to the harbour now inaccessible because of silting.*

Fig. 3 *The modern port of Myrina where Galen would have arrived in the course of his first visit. The castle on the cliff dates to the Byzantine period but the foundation of the settlement was of an earlier date.*

His second attempt to land on Lemnos was well timed so that he could be present on the day of the extraction of the Earth, a ritual carried out by the priestess of Artemis once a year on a set date, the 6th of May. The priestess, followed by a procession, set forth from Hephaistias, the main town in the north part of the island, to the place of extraction, in a cart driven by oxen; she returned to the temple on the same day and subsequently proceeded to wash the Earth herself separating the coarse from the fine materials; she then shaped the Earth into pellets of clay and stamped them with the sign of a goat, the sacred animal of the patron goddess (Artemis). By the end of that visit Galen not only had ascertained that the red colour did not come from goat's blood but was also thoroughly convinced of the useful properties of Lemnian Earth:

".. I had no hesitation myself in testing the medicine, and I took away twenty thousand seals (δυσμυρίας λαβών σφραγίδας)" (Galen *On Simple Drugs* IX.II.247-8; trans. Brock 1929, 194).

It is not clear why Galen needed to bring back to Rome so many pellets. Was the strength of each pellet rather weak? Were his illustrious clients prone to recurring snake bites, or was Galen commissioned to bring back such quantities for the use of the Roman army? Or was it because, as has

5

been suggested (Mayor 2006), fear of poisoning from any source was so prevalent in antiquity that effective antidotes were always in high demand. We shall never know. What is, however, certain is that Galen, with his visit to Lemnos and dispatch to Rome of thousands of pellets, put his own 'stamp' of approval on this medical substance, thus securing its reputation until the end of the 19th century. Its extraction, the pagan ritual observed and reported by him, was overtaken in later times by the Church for the benefit of the island's Ottoman rulers. There are actually eyewitness accounts that it was still practiced in 1918 (Sealy 1919).

Lemnian Earth was very important to the people of antiquity, but does Lemnian Earth exist today? Where and in what form? Is it simply a clay to be extracted from the 'right' location? Or is it the product of some low-level industrial processing? Assuming it could be recovered, would it actually work as a remedy for snake bites and how and why? Can ancient medicines like Lemnian Earth which form part of an intangible heritage acquire an archaeological identity as archaeological artifacts, on a par with ceramics and metals, despite the fact that they are scarcely visible in the archaeological record?

In attempting to address these questions, this book presents the summary of our work on Lemnian Earth and other earths of the Aegean. Earths can be thought of as the industrial minerals of antiquity given the diversity of their applications in everyday life as medicines or mordants, pigments or cleaning agents, cosmetics or fumigants. Many islands in the Aegean (Fig. 1a) including Lemnos, Kimolos, Melos, Samos, Kea, Chios and Euboea, islands usually with volcanic rocks and soils, had their own resources of these primarily clay-based minerals which were sold under the island's name, with different grades of purity and for different applications.

Although it was possible for the same type of earth to be found in more than one island, each island probably developed a different niche market. Some earths became well-known and sought after well beyond the Aegean, while others had already faded into obscurity by the end of antiquity, on account of being replaced by other materials or processes, or simple lack of interest/ resources for their extraction. Table 1 follows Dioscorides' list of the main earths of the Aegean and gives their island of origin and their main applications. Apart from earths, the table includes other mineral substances, such as alum, *miltos, ambelitis, pnigitis* and sulphur. Some earths have also been called *creta (Greek, κρητίς),* perhaps as a means of differentiating them from an earth on the basis of a particular characteristic property (usually white fine powder) or application, as in *creta argentaria* or Kimolian Earth. But why revisit Lemnian Earth, and the earths of the Aegean in general, and

6

why now? We believe there are a number of reasons that make this reassessment topical. First, because, despite extensive documentation, the actual compositions of earths have been elusive. Were they simply raw materials like lumps of clay or were they processed substances? So far the earths of the Aegean have been largely sought through the documentary sources rather than in the field; it therefore follows that, if they are to become more visible in the archaeological record, a combined geological/archaeological approach might be more suitable. It is largely geothermal processes that have given rise to many of these materials, both on Lemnos and elsewhere, and their origin needs to be examined in the context of their respective island's geology. Field walking, geological sampling and analysis and archaeological survey are aspects of field work that are essential in complementing as well as assessing critically the documentary sources.

The second reason is because we wish to investigate whether Lemnian Earth can exist outwith the documentary record; whether it can bear the test of scientific enquiry and, if so, would it be of any use to the modern world? It is only recently that the impacts of geological materials and processes on human health have begun to be scrutinised more closely through the emerging subject of medical geology (Bunnell *et al.* 2007) and the effects of clays as healing substances in the folklore of many cultures (Reinbacher 2003); our own research into the earths of the Aegean, which begun about ten years ago, did so with the purpose of raising awareness for these materials and for the implications of their presence in the lives of people in antiquity (Photos-Jones *et al.* 1997; 1999; Hall *et al.* 2003a; 200b; Photos-Jones and Hall *in press*).

In the last five years there has been a veritable explosion of interest in the medicinal properties of clay minerals. One of the reasons is the emerging need to use clays as potentially new antibacterial agents since the number of organic-based antibiotic-resistant pathogenic bacteria has substantially increased within the last 50 years. Haydel and her co-researchers (Haydel *et al.* 2008, 359) have argued that since "*natural geological minerals harbour antibacterial properties, (they) should provide impetus for exploring ..(new) sources for the presence of novel therapeutic compounds*". Clays are complex materials and ultimately their efficacy may rely not only on the relative ratio between the main ingredients (both active and inert), but also the conditions, internal or external, under which they were applied.

As mentioned earlier, earths have a variety of applications as pigments, mordants or cleansing agents. Perhaps there is less need to revisit pigments and cleansing agents since both groups have long been superseded by a large number of versatile alternatives, both natural and synthetic. Earths of the Aegean and other materials that served as pigments, mordants or cleansing agents are primarily of historical and archaeological interest to islands of their origin and during specific periods. However, earths with medicinal applications constitute an area of research with potentially more far-reaching implications. So in summary, seeking to revisit Lemnian Earth and particularly those earths with medicinal properties is timely because (i) in our view there is a need to remove these substances from the realm of the intangible and the exclusive domain of the documentary record and to try to give them physical substance by looking for them in the field, and (ii) there is now a growing interest from the perspective of the biomedical/pharmacological community to examine and assess properties of inorganic materials/clay minerals and their role as antiseptics but also as alternatives to existing organic-based antibiotics. Lemnian Earth may or may not have a role to play, and this book sets out to explore the possibilities.

Earths	Origin	Main use
Alum	Melos	mordant, medical
Ambelitis	unknown	cosmetic, medical
Chian Earth	Chios	cosmetic, skin treatment
Creta Argentaria	Kimolos	polishing metalware
Eretrian Earth	Euboea	pigment, medical
Kimolian Earth	Kimolos	fulling/cleaning cloth
Lemnian Earth	Lemnos	medical
Melian Earth	Melos	white pigment
Miltos	Kea	red pigment
Pnigitis Earth	unknown	medical
Samian Earth	Samos	fulling (*aster*) medical (*collyrion*)
Selinusian Earth	Selinous	cosmetic
Sulphur/sulfur	Melos	fumigant
Tymphaic Earth	unknown	probably gypsum

Table 1: *Earths of the Aegean mainly after Dioscorides as outlined in his Materia Medica Book V, also known as the Herbal.*

Medicines from plants, minerals and earths

Herb-based medicines

In antiquity, attitudes towards health consisted of the truisms that health was highly desirable, disease a great evil and death the worst lot of mankind (Sigerist 1961, 20). Disease was inflicted by the gods. Every ailment that was not induced by injury was attributed to an act of God and thus beyond the power of man to remedy: *"dietetics was unknown to these early doctors since the internal diseases were a concern of religion rather than of medicine"* Sigerist (1961, 23).

Yet some division of specialisation between physician and surgeon is perhaps reflected in the practices of the two main 'doctors' in the *Iliad* (2.729-733), Machaon and Podalirios. They were the sons of Asklepios, who in the Homeric poems is not the god of healing but a King just like Agamemnon or Menelaus; in a world where all heroes have a basic knowledge of how to treat their wounds in battle, the two brothers, who led their own army against Troy, were particularly skilled in the art. In Homer, medicines (*pharmaka*) were characterized by many adjectives, their meaning often contradictory. They were primarily divided into three groups: (a) those that were benevolent; (b) those that were malevolent; and (c) those with mind-altering properties.

The first group, *pharmaka ipia* or *odynifata*, included plant extracts which were good at soothing the pain or acting as painkillers; the second group, *pharmaka androphona* or *thymophthora*, were considered evil, baneful, accursed, murderous and life-destroying; finally the third group, *pharmaka lygra*, used extracts from plants that affected the brain (Skaltsa 2001).

Some drugs in Homer, particularly those belonging to the third group, are mentioned by name. One such drug which has not yet been identified with any particular plant is the *nepenthes* (*Odyssey* 4.221): Helen of Troy, back in her palace at Argos with her first husband, Menelaus, pours the drug into the wine of visiting Telemachos and of those attending his audience with her husband; Telemachos has come to enquire after the whereabouts of his father Odysseus and the memories of the events retold bring pain and tears to many present. In administering the drug, Helen's aim is *"... to quiet all pain and strife, and bring forgetfulness of every ill"*.

Another drug is the one offered by Circe to Odysseus called *kykeon*

9

(Odyssey 10.234) which consisted of wine, barley meal, and goat's cheese; she added honey to remove the bitter taste of a particular component. The nature of that poisonous extract was not mentioned presumably because only she knew the ingredients. To counter the effect of Circe's drink, Odysseus took from the god Hermes yet a third drug, the extract from a plant called *moly (Odyssey* 10.305). Its root was black but the flowers were milky white. It was hard for mortal men to dig the plant but *'with the gods, all things are possible'*. This plant has been identified as *galanthus nivalis* or the common snowdrop (Plaitakis and Duvoisin 1983), but other plants have also been considered like white hellebore *(Veratrum album)* which has a highly poisonous root and white flowers (Rauber-Lüthy *et al.* 2010). Theophrastus *(Enquiry into Plants* 9.15) knew about it as well and said that it grew on Mount Kyllene in the western Peloponnese.

Homer makes no mention of earths or other mineral substances used in the treatment of wounds, but does report that bandages *(sphendone)* were made from well-twisted sheep's wool *(Iliad* 23.600). Overall, it is suggested that Homeric *pharmaka* were plant-based powders with an astringent or styptic effect; they had a soothing effect, and they lessened the pain and dried out the wound which is just what an astringent would do. When Patroclus rubs a root between his hands and applies it to a wound, Sigerist (1961, 28) speculates that this root may have been an 'onion' since we know that onions have not only an astringent but also a bactericidal effect.

This division of *pharmaka* into the three groups mentioned above merely represents the beginnings of *pharmacognosy*, or the study of medicines derived from natural sources. Early medicine and *pharmacognosy* walked parallel paths. In the Hellenistic period, post-Hippocrates and before Galen and Dioscorides, a number of doctors were prominent in Alexandria, and one presumes beyond, including Herophilos (3rd century AD) (von Staden 1989) and Erasistratos (Fraser 1969); these doctors introduced new elements both to the existing Hippocratean *corpus* and to the priesthood-driven practices associated with healing centres dedicated to Asklepios, like that in Epidaurus, in the eastern Peloponnese. In the same period, *pharmacognosy* rested with medicinal plant-gatherers and dispensers, the *rhizotomoi*, who were involved in the collection of roots and the cultivation of medicinal herbs. Krateuas was a well-known *rhizotomos*, and court physician to Mithridates VI, King of Pontus of the 1st century BC. Krateuas was thought of very highly by Dioscorides for his knowledge of plants and the fact that he chose to illustrate his own herbal, now lost, with very life-like illustrations thereof. Dioscorides speaks respectfully of him in the preface to his *'Herbal'*, although commenting that he (Krateuas) did omit *"many exceptionally useful roots and a few herbs"* (Singer 1927).

Apart from the *rhizotomous*, which were apparently the subject of a now lost play by Sophocles, there were a number of other individuals involved in the extraction, preparation, trade, sale and administration of these materials. Harris (2002, 95) lists a number of associated trades: *pharmakopoles*, a druggist or apothecary mentioned in Aristophanes (*Clouds* 767) and *pharmakotrives*, a drug and/or pigment grinder. There were also *pharmakides* again mentioned in Aristophanes (*Clouds* 750), a woman who collected and administered plants and *rhizopoles*, perhaps a wholesaler in medicinal roots. It is difficult to be certain about the dividing line between the different trades. One interesting point is that the verb *pharmasso* means to treat by using *pharmaka* but also to dye/colour wool (Liddell and Scott 1879). The fact that pigments and *pharmaka* were ground and packaged within the *same* premises may explain why Pliny opted to discuss them together in his *Natural History* XXXV. Finally there is an additional noun, *pharmakos*, which was the name given to a human scapegoat, the unhappy, poor and deformed individual sacrificed or stoned or expelled from the city gates, as part of a religious expiating ceremony (Burkert 1985, 82). The unusual choice of word and the strange 'custom' that went with it has the same root as *pharmaka* but with a different meaning.

Beyond the Homeric drugs known by name in early literature, there are some well-recorded remedies against poisons, one of them being caled *mithridatum*. Mithridates VI is purported to have made himself immune to poison by preparing a concoction of his own, the *mithridatum,* perhaps with the help of his physician Krateuas, the *rhizotomos* mentioned earlier. Celsus *(De Medicina* V.23.3) claims that the King's concoction consisted of thirty six ingredients, thirty four of which were plant-based and the other two were honey and castor (beaver musk); Pliny (*Nat. Hist.* XXIX.25) gives another recipe for *mithridatum* consisting of fifty four ingredients. It is from Pliny (*Nat. Hist.* XXV.6-7) that we know that Mithridates drank poison daily after first taking remedies to achieve immunity and from Cassius Dio's (XXXVII.13) vivid account that, as a result, the King was unable to carry out his own suicide.

Galen (*On Simple Drugs* I.1; Brock 1929, 196) also speaks of *mithridatum* as well as *theriac*, an improvement on *mithridatum* by Andromachus, physician to the emperor Nero; he improved the formula by adding flesh of vipers and increasing the amount of opium. The addition of snake flesh must have derived from the assumption that since some animals appear to be immune to their own poison that immunity must be transferable (Norton 2006). After investigating each of the thirty ingredients in *mithridatum*, the American pharmacologist Norton (2006, 66) concludes that "*there is no convincing evidence from the past that mithridatum was either useful or useless as a remedy for some conditions*".

In examining attitudes towards *pharmaka* in antiquity, it transpires that in the early literature (Homeric poems) *pharmaka* are both malevolent and benevolent, that is, they can both cure as well as poison, and of course they are almost exclusively plant-based; however, in the Classical period *pharmaka* are conceived as either poisons or antidotes to poisons, with the latter usually sweet smelling, a necessary criterion to countenance the bitterness of the former. Homer's mind-altering *pharmaka* feature less prominently in the later periods.

Clays and *Geophagia*

The knowledge and power of 'healing' clays is well embedded in many cultures. To better understand clays in relation to 'earths', brief notes on 'clay' are included (see box below on 'clays') first because this scientific term, an almost everyday word, is used in so many ways that a strict definition is difficult, and second because, as is shown below, one needs to be aware of the complexity of clay minerals and the methodology of their study. It is a 'clay' that the priestess of Artemis processed in Galen's time, and how she did it is critical to our understanding of the nature of Lemnian Earth as well as the other earths.

Clays have been taken internally as a cure of gastrointestinal problems and have been applied externally as poultices to reduce inflammation and fight skin infections. But they have also been ingested deliberately in a practice, observed in both animals and humans and across many cultures and periods ,called *geophagia* or the deliberate and regular eating of earths (Wilson 2003, 1525; Ferrell *et al*. 2009). Whether this is a manifestation of aberrant behavior or a result of fulfilling a particular need is presently the subject of much on-going investigation (Young 2011). Some animals display the same behaviour believed to be a means of neutralizing the effects of toxins within their food (Gilardi *et al*. 1999). *Allotriophagia* (or pica), a type of *geophagia*, is the eating of 'other' unnatural or non-nutritive substances (Dominy *et al*. 2004). While pica is treated as a psychiatric disorder, the reasons for *geophagia,* at least in humans, may not be psychological (Woywodt and Kiss 2002). *Geophagia* first appears in Hippocrates (*On Illnesses* 4.55) but the word used is *geotragia* and not *geophagia.*

An account of the practice of *geophagia* in the New World is given by the explorer Alexander von Humboldt in the late 18th century as he observed the Ottomac Indians of Venezuela. He actively researched the phenomenon and reported on his finds. The geophagic substances appear to have had no nutritive value and the practice was not restricted to the Ottomacs only.

Geophagia appeared to relieve the pangs of hunger in times of famine but it was practised carefully and not indiscriminately (Wilson 2003, 1526). Current attempts by medical doctors, psychologists, ethnographers, sociologists and fiction writers to document and explain this habit have brought *geophagia* to the forefront of public awareness and medical research again. Based on their work in poor areas of urban south Africa, Woywodt and Kiss (2002) suggest that *geophagia* is re-emerging and *"might be triggered by events such as famine, cultural change or psychiatric disease"*. They quote the Colombian writer Gabriel Garcia Màrquez who in his book *One Hundred Years of Solitude* poignantly describes *geophagia* in a woman who is madly in love: "*Rebecca got up in the middle of the night and ate handfuls of earth in the garden with a suicidal drive, weeping with pain and fury, chewing tender earthworms and chipping her teeth on snail shells*" (quoted in Woywodt and Kiss 2002,146).

Oikonomopoulou (2005) describes the old custom of *allotriophagia* among peasant Greek women or those from poor backgrounds and suffering from chronic malnutrition taking place during the first and the last twelve weeks of pregnancy. These women would seek and eat dirty and odd foods, some of them bordering on the disgusting. Traditional midwives and the society at large approved of this 'unhealthy' behaviour on the grounds that it was for the benefit of the baby to be born. Although the women who practiced it are understood to have suffered from 'a psychopathological personality', Oikonomopoulou (2005) argues that *"through it (this practice) the embryo could absorb necessary inorganic elements, which are highly important for its physiological growth"*. It was Covel who travelled to Lemnos in the 17th century and who first reported on the ingestion by Lemnian women of Lemnian Earth to facilitate childbirth and alleviate disorders of menstruation (Covel in Tourptsoglou-Stephanidou 1986, 161).

The reasons why humans appear to have used and consumed earths for medicinal or other purposes are complex and lie at the interface between, on the one hand, rigorous and scientifically observed facts regarding the nature of clays and, on the other, the nebulous sphere of personal and culturally embedded belief systems regarding health and well-being; child-bearing; and attitudes towards illness and how to prevent it. Current scientific literature focuses on case studies, but as mentioned earlier no single parameter emerges as the leading cause behind eating of clays. Wilson (2003, 1525) provides a comprehensive synthesis of the mineralogy of the clays involved in both animal and human *geophagia* and concludes that there is no single explanation for the eating of soils or earths by animals or humans, but a number of hypotheses can be put forward including the following: (a) detoxification or enhancement of palatability of foods which would otherwise be considered unpalatable; (b) the alleviation of diarrhoea; (c) to provide nutritional supplement and with particular reference to iron and calcium; and finally (d) as an antacid to relieve excess acidity.

He also suggests that the tendency to correlate the practice of *geophagia* with clay composition is a natural one, but it may be the case that there is no strict relationship. On the contrary, it may be that some of the properties of the clays rather than their composition may be more relevant; these properties may include bacteriostasis, the temporary stop to the growth of bacteria instigated by the presence of an agent, sterilisation, membrane coating and adsorption of toxins (Wilson 2003, 1545). What is the interaction between clays and bacteria, and can clays be used to control bacterial populations? Clay particles have large surface areas on account of their very small particle size; they also have high cation exchange capabilities and can take up or release toxins or nutrients. Some clays can exchange cations which have antibacterial properties like silver, zinc and copper; these are released slowly enhancing the effectiveness of the clays. Furthermore, clays which can be quite similar can have quite different effects on microbes.

There have been various reasons given as to why different species of animals consume clays. Gilardi *et al.* (1999) observed parrots and concluded that the main reason for parrots consuming 'soils' with a large content of fine clays is because of their ability to absorb toxins. Houston *et al.* (2001) considered similar benefits to elephants and, as in the case of parrots, it seems likely that removal of toxins, and thus increasing the diversity of the potential diet, is the main benefit. As well as clays, earths can contain essential elements like calcium, potassium, magnesium, iron and zinc. The need to provide the body with these chemicals because of an inherent deficiency in the diet is well documented and it may be the reason behind clay consumption. The difficulty in obtaining appropriate samples for investigating *geophagia* is emphasised by Mahaney and Krishnamani (2003) who also provide an extensive review of the topic. Kaolinite is the most common mineral used in *geophagia* followed by smectites and in particular montmorillonite, which is both applied externally for skin infections as well as ingested for gastrointestinal ailments.

In the case of Lemnian Earth, effectiveness in absorbing toxins would be greater the smaller the particle size of the bulk material and the greater the content of expanding smectitic clay i.e. montmorillonite. As mentioned, the small particle size of clays increases dramatically their surface area. Thus, it is on a nano-particle level that one needs to address these issues and appropriate instrumentation is needed to that effect. Clay minerals have the advantage of being able to be applied locally which is preferred to the administering of drugs that are taken internally with potential harmful side effects. The above discussion serves as a background to current research in the properties of medicinal clays. In the sections that follow we shall argue that earths and their properties go beyond those of clays in the sense that earths are composite materials made up of clays as well as other minerals whose properties must have a role to play in the earths' function, whether as pigments or medicines; astringency is one such property.

CLAYS

In everyday use, the word 'clay' is usually taken to mean a fine-grained mud, an unconsolidated sediment. Indeed, it has long been considered geologically to be a sediment, or the portion of any sediment or rock, with a dominant particle size of 2 microns or less, although some authors say less than 4 and others less than 10 microns. Such small particles could not be identified until the advent of powder X-ray diffraction spectrometry (XRD) at the beginning of the 20th century; the 'clay size fraction' of a mud/silt was known to consist of virtually any type of material (mineral, rock, organic, crystals or amorphous material) but these were largely unidentifiable. With the advent of XRD, it was discovered that the dominant constituents of many clays were small crystals of hydrated mineral silicates that had a layered structure. Some of these minerals could also occur in some geological settings as large crystals, much larger than 10 microns but when ground to less than 10 microns or so, had the same XRD profile as the clay examples. Some had a simple composition and relatively simple atomic structure, but many were more complex with a variable chemical composition and atomic structure. Eventually, the word 'clay mineral' became almost synonymous with layered silicate clay' at least in the geological world. The layered silicate clays have now been studied thoroughly and there is a nomenclature and classification approved by the International Mineralogical Association (Brindley and Brown 1980). Layered silicate clay minerals, despite having mineral names, are so complex that it is usually only possible, using routine XRD, to allocate the phases present in a sample to a major group. For example, kaolinite is one of several minerals which belong to the kaolin group. The kaolin group has the main characteristic of an interlayer spacing of about 7 Å. Because XRD analysis is based mainly on characterising clays using their basal interlayer spacings, there has been a move to name them, at least provisionally during identification, on the basis of that spacing i.e. 7 Å clay, etc. This is particularly useful and appropriate in cases where different clay minerals have the same interlayer spacing and much work would have to be undertaken to name the particular clay mineral.

Kaolin is a common clay mineral known commercially as china clay. It is an hydrated alumino-silicate with a relatively simple chemical composition, $Al_2S_{i2}O_5(OH)_4$. It is a major component of potter's clay providing both plasticity and a white colour. It is relatively inert and one of its major modern uses is as a white filler, for example in paper. It can absorb water and other substances such as ink but it is not as powerful an absorbent as montmorillonite/bentonite. The atomic structure of kaolin is relatively simple and is in the form of distinct layers with an interlayer spacing of c. 7 Å which result in a diffraction peak which is readily detected using powder X-ray diffraction, so even very small (clay-size) particles of kaolin can be readily identified. The regularity of the kaolin atomic structure is destroyed on heating to c. 600°C, and the 7 Å peak disappears from powder diffraction traces providing a diagnostic test. The layered atomic structure of kaolin results in the crystals being platy and being deposited as oriented platelets from a liquid suspension or paste thus enhancing the covering power and brightness of kaolin when used as a pigment in paint. Kaolin has also had a long-standing pharmaceutical use as an absorbent in a poultice for soft tissue inflammation. It is also used internally as an absorbent for gastro-enteritis (Mehta 2007).

Montmorillonite is an expanding clay and is a name for a group of expanding clays with a basal spacing of about 15Å at normal humidity, $(Na,Ca)_{0.3}(Al,Mg)_2S_{i4}O_{10}(OH)_2.nH_2O$. Montmorillonite can be calcium or sodium-rich. Fine sediments or rocks which are rich in montmorillonite usually result from the alteration of igneous rocks such as volcanic ashes and are known as bentonite or Fuller's earth. Smectite is the group name favoured by the International Mineralogical Association for the expanding clays.

Non-expanding clays include chlorite, a magnesium and iron-rich layered aluminous silicate mineral; it is often found in altered volcanic rocks and in metamorphic rocks such as schists. It is also found in sediments and clays. It has a 14Å interlayer spacing.

Illite is a 10 Å, clay fraction muscovite-like mineral with a very variable chemical composition. It is non-expanding but may contain layers of expanding smectite clay (a mixed-layer clay). Illite is a common clay component of fine sediments and soils.

Earths

The earths of the Aegean are discussed in varying detail in the works of Theophrastus (*On Stones*), Dioscorides (*De Materia Medica* V), Pliny (*Natural History* XXXV), and Galen (*On Simple Medicines*). But earths must have been used well before the 4th century BC when Theophrastus first reported on them (*On Stones* 62). Theophrastus' father is purported to have been a fuller, and it is assumed that the son would at some stage have had first-hand experience of Kimolian Earth, used for the degreasing of wool. Regarding the Earth's medicinal applications which Theophrastus barely mentions, these may have developed as an afterthought, a chance trial with beneficial results. Or perhaps it was the other way round; we can only speculate. What is of interest is that most earths have some medicinal properties but it was Lemnian, Samian (the *collyrion* variety) and Eretrian Earths that were the most effective ones; Kimolian Earth and the second type of Samian Earth (*aster*) were used by fullers in the degreasing of wool. Melian Earth and Keian *miltos* were used as white and red pigments, and alum and sulphur as mordant and fumigant respectively. But how were earths defined?

For Galen an earth was *"the name commonly given by all Greeks to that which, when put into water, instantly dissolves and turns into mud (πηλός). That used in agriculture has certain varieties, a greasy and sticky kind being quite dark in colour, while another kind, not fatty, but more friable, is called white clay (ἀργυλος) this having a whitish tint. These are the extreme varieties, and the other earths are between them, approaching either the one or the other..."* (Galen *On Simple Drugs* IX.II; trans. Brock 1929, 196). By calling these substances earths, Galen presumably understood that they were basically clays or fine-grained materials aimed to enhance the properties of the soils but that only one variety of them was used in agriculture. He adds a word of caution:

"it will be necessary to distinguish medicinal earth from that used in agriculture. There could be no greater mistake than to give this latter name to that which we use in medicine, although the fatty part even of agricultural soil is useful in the treatment of all parts needing dessicative treatment." (Galen *On Simple Drugs* IX.II; trans. Brock 1929, 195).

Dioscorides' book on medical substances (*De Materia Medica*), often referred to in English as *The Herbal*, is the first manual containing information on many substances with therapeutic properties primarily plant-based.

Although Theophrastus' (*Enquiry into Plants* and *On the causes of Plants*) was the first to attempt a formal classification of plants, he was less interested than Dioscorides in their medicinal properties. The *Herbal* is divided into five books: Book I is on aromatic oils, ointments and trees, Book II on animals and cereals, Book III on roots, juices and herbs, Book IV on herbs and roots, and Book V on wines, minerals and earths. It is Book V that is of interest here. The *Herbal* was in continuous use from antiquity to the Renaissance period, enriched in commentaries by both western and eastern sources. In John Goodyear's 'Englished' translation of 1655, based on contemporary editions of Dioscorides' opus, the author acknowledges the illustrations to be by an unknown Byzantine artist sometime in 512 AD. The Goodyear translation was published in 1934 having been edited by Gunther (1934) who retained the antiquated 17th century English. Beck's (2005) recent translation, with commentaries, from the authoritative Wellman text in German dated to the early 20th century, has provided a much needed up-to-date English translation of the great work.

Of over 900 entries in the 'Herbal' nearly 650 are plant-based with the remainder being animal and mineral products, inorganic salts and rocks including alum, sulphur and *miltos*, soot, asphalt, sand, metallic oxides, carbonates, sulphides and slags from the smelting of ferrous and non-ferrous ores and metals. Dioscorides reports on only nine earths, but the fact that earths are included in his *Herbal* in the first place suggests that by the 1st century AD their pharmaceutical applications were well appreciated and their presence in subsequent '*Herbals*' secured. Dioscorides defines earths as *"all earth that falls within the compass of medicinal use (*which*) hath supreme faculty of cooling and stopping the pores, but it differs in kind: one being good for other things with some preparations"* (*De Materia Medica* V.170; edited by Gunther 1934). So although Galen sees earths within the broader context of their many applications based on physical attributes like colour and texture, Dioscorides focuses solely on those "that fall within the compass of medicinal use*"*.

Discussing earths on the basis of their properties/applications was the preferred way ancient writers addressed these materials. Pliny writes *"we have discussed the properties of earths as medicines elsewhere and now we will deal with them as paints"* (*Nat. Hist.* XXXV.20). He does exactly that and practically in the same sentence. In reference to *miltos* (*Nat. Hist.* XXXV.32) he writes *"It is used for the painting of the base of the wall, in medicine it is prescribed to relieve pain"*, seemingly confident that the reader will not be wondering how the same substance can simultaneously be taken internally as well as being used to paint onto a wall. This association between paints and medicines has been reflected in the trade and with regards to *pharmakotrives,* as mentioned earlier. This seamless transition in the classical authors' discussion of earths as either paints or cleansing agents or pharmaceuticals has generated a host of questions; it has also been open to many (mis-) interpretations in the ensuing centuries as to the exact nature of these materials and their mineralogical composition. 'Manuals' such as Agricola's *De Re Fossilium* (1546) and *De Re Metallica* (1556) revealed to the public the then newly found knowledge of inorganic metallic and non-metallic substances as they were emerging from the mines of central Europe and with it the desire to revisit, understand and reinterpret the relevant classical texts. With the establishment of scientific (wet chemical) analysis in the mid-19th century these substances got their last chance to be technically characterized before their use and the memory of their use became obsolete.

Stephanides (1898) produced a dense and thorough critique of Theophrastus' 'mineralogy' (*On Stones*). Stephanides, a state chemist from the island of Lesvos in the North Aegean, at that time still under Ottoman rule, was a fervent believer in the way that Greek thought and practice influenced modern scientific thought. What is not clear is how he ascribed particular mineralogical terms to individual earths with such an air of authority and conviction and at a time before the discovery of x-rays and the widespread use of the x-ray diffractometer. We can only presume that the formula for each earth was generated on the basis of wet chemical analysis alone but also that he had access to samples of these earths and, of course, that he was confident that these earths were the 'same' as those used in antiquity.

Stephanides' work is little known outside Greece, but for the English- speaking world, widely referenced are: the works of Eichholtz (1965) and Caley and Richards (1956) on Theophrastus' *On Stones*; Eichholtz (1962) on Pliny's treatise of stones; Bailey (1929 and 1932) on Pliny's chemical substances; Levidis (1994) on Plinys treatise of pigments for artists; and Healy (1999) on Pliny's 'science'. These publications have made the writings of the early technical authors available to both classicists as well as scientists. Regarding Dioscorides, there are the translations by Goodyear (Gunther 1934) and Beck (2005) and also the extensive commentary by Riddle (1985). These investigators scrutinized the texts and relied on knowledge of 20th century mineralogy, and their own experiments (when they did carry them out) to come up with the 'best fit' regarding the mineralogy of each earth - hence the often different opinions as to the composition of each earth. The point here is not to assess who might have been 'right' or 'wrong' but to steer the investigation away from the documentary sources (and their interpretation) and into the field, as an alternative approach to the study of the earths. Regarding Lemnian Earth there are two major recent accounts by Tourptsoglou-Stephanidou (1986) and Paximadas (2002). The former puts the Earth in the context of travellers' descriptions of the island as a whole; the latter by a medical man, with a local practice in the island's main hospital over the previous thirty years, and considerable insight and with understanding of 'things Lemnian' brings forward lesser known doctors of antiquity and later periods, emphasizing both symptoms and cures and from a doctor's perspective. Both books provide a rich and in-depth presentation of the relevant literature.

Although by far the most well known of the medicinal earths, Lemnian Earth was not the only one. There were others from localities outside the Aegean such as: that from Malta which was thought to have been prescribed by the eminent 15th century alchemist/doctor, Paracelscus (Dannenfeldt 1984, 175); that from the Middle East (*Terra of Bethlehem*) (Hasluck and Hasluck 1929); and *Terra Silesia* from Poland; that all made an appearance in the 15th century, probably as a means of filling the void created by the diminishing confidence in the efficacy of Lemnian Earth. Up to an additional thirty earths appeared between the 16th and the 18th centuries from various places in Central Europe including Hungary and Bohemia, riding on the back of Lemnian Earth's acclaimed fame (Dannenfeldt 1984, 188) and taking advantage of its potential adulteration with other earths of lesser quality. In the meantime *terra sigilata,* or stamped earth, the original name ascribed to Lemnian Earth, became the generic name for all stamped materials with pharmaceutical applications.

Up until the mid 1970s, and with the exception of Pittinger (1975), no one had actually sought earths systematically in the field. Her pioneering study in Melos in the Cyclades (Fig. 1) formed the springboard on which to base our own team's work on the same island and beyond in later years (Photos-Jones *et al*. 1999; McNulty 2000; Hall *et al*. 2003a, b; Photos-Jones and Hall in *press*). Understanding the nature of local 'clays', the local geology and the geological/geochemical processes active in the locality, where a particular earth was thought to have been extracted, lies at the heart of any future investigation of earths. The choice of the landscape on which to focus the investigation is the outcome of more than an educated guess, since localities of exploitation could well have changed over time, as could have the colour, texture, applications and efficacy of the extracted material.

As well as a knowledge of the local geology, an understanding is required of on-site and off-site possible enrichment processes. There is little information in the texts regarding post-extraction processing and yet this is one aspect that merits further consideration. The enrichment and further processing of clays and earths, if ever took place, often involved dissolution in water, evaporation of water and recrystallisation, all taking place at low temperatures, probably about 100°C. This environmentally friendly industrial process, however, leaves little waste that can be clearly differenti-ated from the raw material; thus the task of searching for raw material, product and waste in an ancient mining or processing site becomes even more difficult.

Earths, although basically clays, did not consist of pure clay minerals; rather, they were composite materials made up of clay and other minerals, all components contributing to the nature/properties of the final product. It is inevitable that if one or more components predominated (percentage wise), either naturally or *via* beneficiation, then this fact would render the earth, the product, more suitable for one application as opposed to another. On the other hand, for the medicinal earth to be effective that component may have been quite small. What our work has highlighted is that it is un-wise to examine earths on mineralogical terms alone but rather as industrial minerals whose properties rather than their composition is the driving force behind their applications. This indeed is the attitude that ancient writers like Pliny, for example, have taken all along.

Are any samples of Lemnian Earth available for examination today? There are indeed some samples in private mineral collections, such as for example that of Sir Hans Sloane at the Natural History Museum in London (Sweet 1935, 147; Macgregor 1994). Much of the content of Sweet's article is on Sloane's box of 'minerals' that included Lemnian and Samian Earths. One of the drawers representing the 'mineral pharmaceutical collection' and con-taining the samples of Lemnian Earth was seen in 2000 by one of us (AJH) (Fig. 4). It can be argued that any museum samples, even those in important historical collections such as the Sloane Collection, need not represent 'true' Lemnian Earth, as of the type obtained by Galen. But then, could there be such thing as one 'true' Lemnian Earth? There is an additional point to be made. We assume that earths worked because their composition and properties were suitable for the treatment of specific ailments, and not that they worked simply because the ancient world *believed* them or *willed* them to work. Earth, the archaeological artefact, must have been basically,

 but not uniquely, clay, and how the different components interacted once ingested or applied will take a lot more than an archaeological guide to resolve.

Fig. 4 *Sir Hans Sloane's 'box of miner-als' as photographed by AJH in 2000. The collection was described by Sweet (1935).*

Lemnian Earth: related myths

The earliest reference to the healing properties of Lemnian Earth is firmly embedded within the cycle of poetry associated with the Homeric poems, the Trojan War and its main participants, and in particular, the hero Philoctetes (*Iliad* 2.718-725); Philoctetes, although setting off with the rest of the Greek army to fight at Troy, was left behind on the island of Lemnos, on account of having been bitten by a water snake, his wound festering and emanating a malodorous smell (see brief account of myth below).

Homer thought that Lemnos was Hephaistos' 'most beloved land' ('*Λήμνος γαιάων πολύ φιλτάτη ...απασέων*') (*Odyssey* 8.284). In antiquity many adjectives were ascribed to Lemnos, like the cloudy one (*αμιχθαλόεσσα*) (*Iliad* 24.753). Other names like sooty (*αιθάλεια*) or fiery (*πυρόεσσα*), both alluding to her perceived volcanic activity, have been used; it was also thought to be full of vineyards (*αμπελούσα*).

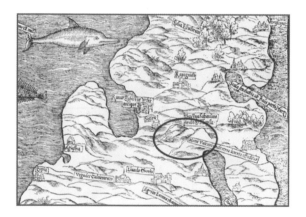

Fig. 5 *Detail of Belon's 16th century map (1588) depicting the Mons Vulcani, or Mosychlos, where Lemnian Earth was extracted (unde terra lemnia effoditur). Note the three hills, circled, and the pannier with Lemnian Earth, exaggerated in scale. The chapel of Aghios Sotiras (St Saviour) is also depicted to the left as are the ruins of Hephaistias (Ephestiae); also shown are Ayiasma, and the village of Rapanidi. Compare with Fig. 7.*

There are four separate clusters of myths surrounding mythical figures and events that are integrally associated with Lemnian Earth. First, **Hephaistos**, the god of natural and artificially produced fire, patron of craftsmen, builders and metalworkers, and his relationship to Lemnos on which he is purported to have landed after being jettisoned by his father, Zeus, from Mount Olympus; it is on Lemnos that he kept (one of) his workshop(s)

22

(*Iliad* 1.593). Then there is **Philoctetes**, his trials and tribulations on account of the snake bite and his crucial role in the outcome of the war at Troy; third, the set of myths associated with the story of the **Lemnian fire** (*Λήμνιον Πύρ*) (Sophocles *Philoctetes* 800; Aristophanes *Lysistrata* 299) that was tended by his priests; it was these same priests who, according to Eustathius (see below), were the dispensers of Lemnian Earth; finally, there are two sets of myths associated with the first and second **Lemnian crimes** *(Λήμνια κακά)* (Herodotus *Histories* VI.138) recounting the events of the slaughter of Lemnian men by their (Lemnian) women (first crime) and the subsequent slaughter, on Lemnos, of Athenian women and their sons by their (Lemnian) men (second crime). Given the richness of the mythological record we believe we are justified in suggesting that some myths may provide an 'environmental framework' on which geological and anthropogenic events can be pegged and which could underpin our understanding of the healing properties of Lemnian Earth.

Fig. 6 *View from the NW to the silted harbour of Hephaistias; in the background the truncated 'cone' of Kastro Vouni prominent in the adjoining hills, giving the same impression of 'three peaks' as that shown in Belon's map in Fig. 5.*

Hephaistos: Of all the Olympian gods Hephaistos was perhaps the most ungodly. Lame at birth (*Odyssey* 8.267) and deformed, short and generally unattractive, his own mother could not come to terms with his deformity and rejected him. Hera, gave birth to him without the participation of her consort, Zeus (Hesiod, *Theogony* 924). She dispatched him or rather threw him off Mount Olympus to the depths of the sea where the sea nymphs took care of him as he grew up (*Iliad* 18.136). Zeus also gave birth without his wife's assistance to another Olympian, the goddess Athena, who sprang fully armed out of his head. 'Cool' Athena was no basis of comparison with Hephaistos. Her looks, stature, beauty and wisdom set her apart from the rest of the gods. Yet by some accounts it was Hephaistos who delivered the blow on Zeus' head precipitating Athena's birth (Pindar, *Olympian Ode* 7.33).

Hephaistos is perhaps the archetype of the child rejected by his mother who grew up with the hope that one day she would seek him out, admit her 'error' and take him back to Mount Olympus. Indeed a recent play by a modern Scottish playwright delves into this issue by giving it a contemporary perspective (Dolan 2008). But Hera made no such move. Seeing that no such initiative was coming from her, he decided to 'force' events. He built for her a magnificent throne as befitted the queen of gods. She was naturally flattered and suspected no ill doings, yet the moment she sat on it she regretted it bitterly. Invisible chains tied her onto her seat. To her pleading that she should be set free he replied not until she admitted the error of her ways. Eventually it was Dionysus who having made Hephaistos drunk, brought him back to Mount Olympus to set his mother free (Pausanias *Description of Greece* 1.20). For releasing his mother of the chains, Hephaistos also got Aphrodite, the goddess of beauty, as his prize. They married but she duly rejected him by sleeping with Ares, the god of war. Hephaistos again plotted his revenge carefully, as with his mother, by trapping Aphrodite and her lover with an invisible net. He then called all the gods to come and witness the adulterous couple in the act. (*Iliad* 8. 267). The personal life of this 'unhappy' god never really affected his work life as he was after all the patron god of craftsmen particularly those working with a furnace. His craft work was unparalleled having shaped Achilles' armour and shield (*Iliad* 18.136-19.23*)*, the gods' palaces (*Iliad* 1.605), his mother's throne, and automata like the tripods on which the gods sat and which would wheel themselves into place at the time of meetings (*Iliad* 18.136) as well as a famous woman, Pandora (Hesiod *Theogony* 560*)*. His workshop was on Lemnos and thought to be at the base of a hillock, called Mosychlos. The association of Hephaistos and Lemnos may have created a parallel between Vulcan and Mount Etna in Sicily.

Hephaistos was cast off Mount Olympus not once but twice: first by his mother and then by his father Zeus. Hephaistos was rejected by his father Zeus, because in the course of a marital argument between his parents he inevitably took his mother's side. Zeus hurled him from Mount Olympus. He travelled for nine days and nine nights over the sky and eventually landed on Lemnos. There he set up his workshop in the interior of a mythical mount called Mosychlos *(Iliad* 1.568).

Hephaistos' daily routine of working on metals in his workshop in Lemnos has been directly associated with volcanism. From a geological perspective the myth has little justification since there is overwhelming evidence that there has been no volcanic activity during human occupation of Lemnos. While there are rocks of volcanic origin that influence the topography of Lemnos, these rocks are millions of years old and are very unlikely to have been recognized as volcanic rocks until mapped by geologists. We can only infer from this that the Hephaistos myth was re-iterating events in some way reminiscent of volcanic activity like, for example, the burning of fires as a result of hydrocarbon emissions. Hydrocarbon emissions might be directly connected with the Lemnian fire.

Lemnian fire: Lemnian fire appears in Aristophanes: *"Tis Lemnian fire that smokes, or else it would not sting my eyelids thus..."* (Aristophanes, *Lysistrata* 299) and is also invoked in Sophocles' *Philoctetes* (1066) where the eponymous hero looks at burning within it as a solace to the pains he was suffering on account of his wound. The implication is that whatever fire was burning on Lemnos was no ordinary fire but rather one that was far hotter than anything experienced normally in a hearth.

De Launay, a geologist and an amateur archaeologist, subscribed to the idea of burning of hydrocarbons as did some of his contemporaries (Tourptsoglou-Stephanidou 1986, 493). The fact that the Lemnian fire needed to be tended (by the priests of Hephaistos) and that it could disappear without leaving a trace is certainly corroborative evidence to that effect. It is quite clear to De Launay that the Lemnian fire was not present at the time of Galen's visit, otherwise Galen would have commented on it.

The Lemnian fire was associated with the annual festival of the extinction of all fires on Lemnos for nine days during which no forge was in operation and no hearths were lit. For nine days Lemnian women sacrificed to subterranean and other secret deities. To mark the end of the festival a sacred ship brought new fire to Lemnos from Delos. The new fire was then distributed to craftsmen and households, and the island returned to normal life. The arrival of the fire from Delos may have been a later development; previous to that the domestic hearth fires may have been lit from sources within the island, like hydrocarbon emissions which would not be easily extinguished and would be continuous. Hephaistos was also worshipped in Athens in conjunction with Athena at two major festivals: first during the *Chalkeia* when clay statues and plaques of the god were placed next to kilns and domestic hearths, and second during the *Apatouria* when young Athenian males were presented for citizenship (Larson 2007, 159). This litany of myths binding Hephaistos with Lemnos strengthens the view about the island's geothermally active field and its many manifestations.

Regarding the occurrence of **Lemnian crimes**, Herodotus gives the following account:

"These Pelasgians (the Lemnians) dwelt at that time in Lemnos and desired vengeance on the Athenians. Since they well knew the time of the Athenian festivals, they acquired fifty-oared ships and set an ambush for the Athenian women celebrating the festival of Artemis at Brauron. They seized many of the women, then sailed away with them and brought them to Lemnos to be their concubines. These women bore more and more children, and they taught their sons the speech of Attica and Athenian manners. These boys would not mix with the sons of the Pelasgian women; if one of them was beaten by one of the others, they would all run to his aid and help each other; these boys even claimed to rule the others, and were much stronger. When the Pelasgians perceived this, they took counsel together; it troubled them much in their deliberations to think what the boys would do when they grew to manhood, if they were resolved to help each other against the sons of the lawful wives and attempted to rule them already. Thereupon the Pelasgians resolved to kill the sons of the Attic women; they did this, and then killed the boys' mothers also. From this deed and the earlier one which was done by the women when they killed their own husbands who were Thoas' companions, a "Lemnian crime" has been a proverb in Hellas for any deed of cruelty" (Herodotus *Histories* 6.138; trans. Godley 1920).

Philoctetes is the Homeric hero who together with other Greeks set out to take part in the war against Troy. While on Lemnos, or rather the now submerged small island of Chryse, he was bitten by a water snake and was left behind by his comrades on account of the stench of his festering wound. He stayed on Chryse for ten years, embittered and nursing his wound. However, it was decreed that Troy would not fall to the Greeks unless Philoctetes, who was in possession of Heracles' magic arrows, returned to Troy. In Sophocles' play, '*Philoctetes*', Odysseus, who had been instrumental for the hero's involuntary exile, in the first place, returns to Lemnos together with Neoptolemus, the son of Achilles, to try to persuade by trickery the unhappy Philoctetes to come to the aid of the Greeks.

Philoctetes' mental and physical wounds continue to be relevant in our world today. A recent rewrite of the Sophocles play by the Irish author and Nobel prize winner Seamus Heaney, 'The *Cure at Troy*' (Heaney 1996), revisits the theme and explores the conflict between young Neoptolemus' idealism, and Odysseus' realisation of the political necessity of persuading the reluctant hero to join the Greeks and the dishonorable means he uses to that effect.

Why did it take such a long time for Philoctetes' wound to heal? A recent article in the *American Journal of Dermatology* (Farella 1996) attempted to address this question by delving into the symptoms of his disease. It was concluded that the painful and malodorous wound may have started as lesions attributed to *chromoblastomycosis*, a chronic fungal infection of the skin, producing wart-like nodules. These develop in large growths which may multiply over a period of weeks or months often resulting in secondary bacterial infections.

The cult of Hephaistos was widespread in Lemnos. Yet the excavations of the Italian School of Archaeology and the Greek Archaeological Service at the site of Hephaistias, in progress since the late 1920s, have revealed no temple of Hephaistos. It is possible that a cave at or near the vicinity of a mythical hill, called Mosychlos, may have been the base for both worship and healing. Today there is no particular feature under that name, the hillock of Kastro Vouni probably being the one identified with Mosychlos a mythical place name associated with the god (Buttman in Tourptsoglou-Stephanidou 1986, 562). Figure 5 shows Belon's map with the said triple-peak range and the volcano-shaped 'first' peak. The remains of the *'Ephestiae urbis antique'* are also shown, together with the neighbouring village of Repanidi. Figure 6 shows a photo of the triple-peak range from the bay of the site of ancient Hephaistias, while Thevet's map (Fig. 7), dating to the same period, provides an equally 'imaginative' reconstruction of the island's geography (see also details in Figs. 61a-b). Nevertheless, the place names seen in both maps must have all been real places that one could visit in the 16th century.

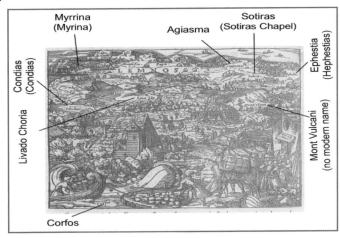

Fig. 7 *Thevet's (1575, 806) map of Lemnos with key place names transcribed for easier reading. Compare with Belon's map in Fig. 5. Ayiasma, Aghios Sotiras, Hephaistias and Mons Vulcani are shown as are Myrina and Condias, suggesting that they were all 'real enough places in the 16th century.*

27

Lemnian Earth: facts

Lemnian Earth, the raw material, was not always referred to by that name. Theophrastus (*On Stones 52*) calls it Lemnian *miltos* (*μίλτος*) rather than Earth and reflects on it merely as a red pigment. In a later section we return to the topic of *miltos*, fine iron oxides, from the island of Kea in the Northern Cyclades and considered by Theophrastus to be the best. The medicinal benefits of Lemnian Earth did not become apparent at least in the literature until the 2nd century BC. Araetaios from Capadocia is the first to mention Lemnian *sphragis*, or troche, (σφραγίς Λημνία) (Araetaios 5, Οξέων νόσων θεραπευτικόν). The word 'troche', often appearing in association with Lemnian Earth, simply means a medicinal tablet of round shape, usually stamped.

Nicander of Colophon, who lived in the 2nd century BC, wrote two poems which survive: *Theriaca* and *Alexipharmaka*. The former describes poisonous creatures, the symptoms of their bites and stings and remedies when the poisons are absorbed via the skin. In *Alexipharmaka* the poisons described are those taken internally and are of different origin, plant, animal or mineral. The book describes the solutions into which they are mixed, the symptoms deriving from these poisons and the appropriate remedies. Inorganic substances in Nicander include *Lemnian Earth* as well as *miltos* and *gagates*, the ancient name for jet (Mottana 2006). Nikander, made the connection between *miltos* and *sphragis*, stating that Lemnian *miltos* is the one they call Lemnian *sphragis* (Nikander *Theriaka* 864). He also described it as καθαρτική (cleansing). Andromachus (1st century AD), personal doctor to the emperor Nero, called Lemnian Earth Lemnian *miltos* (*Λημνιάδος μιλτοίο*) suggesting, like Nikander, that the pigment was red and could be used as a medicine (Andromachus, *Θηριακή δι' εχιδνών*, 147).

It is Dioscorides (*De Materia Medica* V.113) who called this material *Lemnian Earth* (*Λημνία γή*), but he also occasionally refers to it as Lemnian *miltos*. He considers it an 'eminent antidote against deadly poisons when drank with wine'. Dioscorides thought that the red colour was due to the mixing of Lemnian Earth with goat's blood. As already mentioned, Galen originally took his suggestion seriously but subsequently dismissed it during his visit. Given the red colour, Lemnian Earth could well have contained fine-grained red ferric iron oxide, the mineral hematite, but this is unlikely to have been the *dominant* constituent (see discussion on the composition of Lemnian Earth).

28

Terra sigillata is among the various names that Pliny gives to Lemnian Earth that also include *Lemnia rubrica, terra Lemnia* and *terra rubricata* (Pliny *Nat. Hist.* XXXV.14; XXVIII.24; XXIX.33). By calling it *terra rubricata* and by saying (*"it resembles cinnabar"*) it is clear that for Pliny, also, Lemnian Earth was red. It was of course primarily as a medicine that Lemnian Earth acquired its widespread reputation against poisons and snakebites: *"In medicine it was used as an ointment around the eyes to relieve pain and inflammation"* (Pliny *Nat. Hist.* XXXV.14). Pliny describes Lemnian Earth as being an antidote to poisons when poison was already swallowed and against snake bites (*Nat. Hist.* XXIX.33; XXXV.14). It was also used as a treatment for dysentery (*Nat. Hist.* XXVIII.24; XXIX.33, 104; XXXV.14).

Galen calls it *Lemnia rubrica*, Lemnian *miltos* and also Lemnian *sphragis* (Λημνία σφραγίς), qualifying the difference between *miltos* and earth. He says that *"it differs from this* (miltos) *in not leaving a stain when handled"* (Galen *On Simple Drugs* IX, II; trans. Brock 1929, 192). We can infer therefore that Lemnian Earth was not a high-quality pigment but did contain sufficient colorant to make it distinctly red.

Philostratus Flavius, a Lemnian sophist who lived in the 2nd century AD, mentions in his chapter on Philoctetes (*Heroica* VI.2*)* that the priests of Hephaistos cured his wounds with Lemnian bole (βώλου της Λημνίας). However, in Sophocles' version of the Philoctetes myth the eponymous hero's wound did not heal until he arrived in Troy and in his long years of suffering Philoctetes had used a herb, and not a mineral, not available elsewhere but on the island of Lemnos (Sophocles *Philoctetes* 659).

Polyaenus, writing in the 2nd century AD, narrates a story about a Macedonian called Amphiretos who, when captured by pirates, used a fragment of Lemnian Earth which resulted in him urinating blood-red urine. Thinking he was sick, the pirates let him go (Polyaenus, *Strategems* VI).

Philumenus, who lived in the 4th century AD and wrote a treatise on poisonous animals *(De Venenatis Antimalibus Eorumque Remedis)* called Lemnian Earth, Lemnian *shragis* and mentions it as an antidote to poison. During the Byzantine period there are numerous references to Lemnian Earth as pointed out by Paximadas (2002) who lists a considerable number of them, together with the ailments that Lemnian Earth was meant to cure.

Eustathius, Bishop of Thessaloniki, writing in the 12th century AD, in his comments on the *Iliad*, confirmed that the priests of Hephaistos were healing those who had been bitten by snakes (οἱ του Ηφαίστου ιερείς εθεράπευον *τους οφεοδήκτους)* (Tourptsoglou-Stephanidou 1986, 84).

Reference to Lemnian Earth as pigment is given by Vitruvius: "*The red variety too, is extracted in great abundance from many places but the best comes only from a few of them, like Sinope in Pontus, Egypt and the Balearic Islands of Hispania, also Lemnos*" (Vitruvius *On Architecture* VII; trans. Rowland and Noble Howe 1999).

Red was not always the colour of Lemnian Earth but in antiquity it was marketed as a substance of red colour. While the Classical sources agree that Lemnian Earth was red, travellers to the lands of the Ottoman Empire clearly state that it was yellow. Agricola (1530, 215) in his *Bernannus,* gives an account of how the pills were sold in Venice and how he himself sold four pills for 55 ducats, a fairly respectable amount at the time. This is the oldest reference we have on the commercial aspect of Lemnian Earth. He then goes on to mention that the Turks were using Lemnian Earth as the one and only remedy for plague, in the same way as the Arabs were using the Armenian Bole (Tourptsoglou-Stephanidou 1986, 84). When the French naturalist Pierre Belon travelled to Istanbul in the early 16th century he collected small *sphargides* of Lemnian Earth which were of different colours, sizes, weight or stamps suggesting that the original Earth was being adulterated or others were being sold as the real thing (Belon 1588). We will return to the geological parameters that could influence the colour of Lemnian Earth and provide a justification for its variation in a later section.

Galen makes it clear that there are other varieties apart from medicinal Lemnian Earth; one is used as a pigment and "*the third is that which removes dirt, and which can be used, if desired, by those who wash linen and clothes*" (Galen *On Simple Drugs* IX.II.247-8; trans. Brock 1929, 193). There were therefore different 'grades' or 'qualities' of Lemnian Earth distinguished by colour, particle size and mineral inclusions; the 'lower quality' grades were more gritty. The use of Lemnian Earth as a pigment seems to fade after the Roman period due to the almost certain availability of better red-staining substances and the rising reputation of Lemnian Earth as a medicine.

Up to the middle of the 18th century there appear to be very few, if any doubts regarding the curative properties of Lemnian Earth. However, in the late 18th century questions were raised as to whether its therapeutic properties may not be resting simply on the belief that it *does* cure. Daniel Philippides and Gregory Konstandas, two educated Greek clergymen, visiting Lemnos in the late 18th century and present at the site on the day of its extraction, wrote in their diary:

"on the 22nd September ...we saw the hole partly filled up and its soil which was a light coloured clay. It could not possibly have a therapeutic value. Furthermore in the case of fever, when the stomach is weak, it would aggravate the illness which caused it (the fever) in the first place.... " (Gregory Konstandas in Tourptsoglou-Stephanidou 1986, 292).

Earlier travellers, most of them educated men of means, were equally puzzled, but in their own accounts each balanced the pros and cons differently. For example, Belon (1588) was convinced that it was the ritual that gave Lemnian Earth its value, rather than the properties of the material itself. As mentioned, Belon visited Constantinople in 1543 where he encountered eighteen different types of material marketed as Lemnian Earth with different colour, size, and stamps, like that of a cross. It soon became apparent to him that some debasing of the pure material was taking place, for example local traders were mixing it with Arrmenian Bole, another earth. Furthermore, he reports that seal impressions on debased varieties were different to the ones on the true one. Therefore, Belon illustrated these seals in his book for the benefit, as he noted, of the medical world (Belon 1588). Belon also mentions that the Turks clearly differentiated between two types of Earth, *thin –i makhtoum-i ahmer*, i.e. the red earth and the *thin–i makhtoum-i ebiez,* the white earth (Tourptsoglou-Stephanidou 1986, 111), the latter considered of lower quality. The weight of the sealed earth was *c.* 4 drams (i.e. *c.* 8 g).

Semandrida ge (σημαντρίδα γή) is another albeit lesser known name for Lemnian Earth which appeared in a document dated 1480 when the sultan sent medical men to Lemnos to investigate its nature and potential (Tourptsoglou-Stephanidou 1986, 85). Interestingly, according to Liddell and Scott (1879) "*semandrida ge*" was a clay used for sealing, "*like our wax*", first mentioned in Herodotus (Histories 2. 38), in association with a ritual sacrifice of a bull by the Egyptians (De Sélincourt 2003). Finally *ayiochoma* or sacred earth *(αγιόχωμα)* is the name by which most travellers' accounts to the island agree that Lemnians identified Lemnian Earth. Indeed that is how it was referred to us in the course of our first visit to the island in 1998, the name Lemnian Earth being used by a small pottery workshop in the village of Kontopouli and also as a label for a local wine. However there is now sufficient scientific interest on the matter for the material to revert to the name it has been mostly recognised by. Perhaps not surprisingly, the stamping of healing clays with the sign of the cross is a tradition that started with Lemnian Earth but continues to exist to this day. The manufacturing and selling of clay tablets embossed with Indian and Christian symbols referred to as *panito del senor* or small bread of the Lord can be seen in Guatemala and neighbouring Honduras and Mexico, today; it is particularly consumed by pregnant women (Hunter *et al.* 1989).

Lemnian Earth: where to find it

It is almost impossible to know the exact location of the extraction of the earths unless there is some associated documentary evidence. This is the case with Lemnian Earth but not necessarily the rest of the earths. The other earths therefore need to be traced to some geological source compatible with their proposed mineralogy, but if the composition is not known then the area can only be loosely identified. We know little about the location of Samian Earth. This is further complicated by the fact that there were two types of Samian Earth, one medicinal and the other used by fullers. But were both extracted from the same place? Regarding Eretrian Earth there are well documented clay deposits in the Lelantine Plain between Eretria and Chalkis (see Figs. 40, 41). Was this deposit the source of Eretrian Earth?

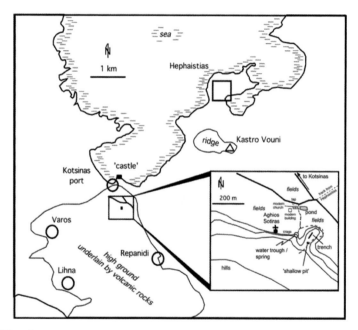

Fig. 8 *The area of Lemnos including Kotsinas and the archaeological site of Hephaistias. For enlarged version of the* inset *see Fig. 16.*

Regarding Lemnian Earth, there are four places which are relevant to the present narrative. They are located in the north of the island as shown in Fig. 8 and include (a) the hamlet of Kotsinas with the scant remains of its medieval castle, (b) the area of the Phtheleidia spring (within the boxed detail, also shown enlarged in Fig. 16) including a number of features within, (c) the archaeological site of Hephaistias (shown with a square) and its environs, and (d) the hill of Kastro Vouni (easternmost part of ridge, shown with a triangle).

These localities form the nodal points in the paths followed by two travellers to Lemnos, whose eye-witness accounts, pertaining to the ritual of the extraction of the Earth, we have in considerable detail. Galen and Belon travelled to this area in search of Lemnian Earth at two different times about fourteen centuries apart. Belon (1588) was a French naturalist and an intrepid traveller whose vivid accounts of life in the Ottoman lands in the mid-16th century form the backbone of what we know of daily life at that period. It is the geological background to the paths the two visitors took that we wish to investigate in order to give our study a historical context and to search for pointers to the existence of the Earth. The following pages are intended to be of use by the reader while on Lemnos and while attempting to retrace their paths. As a result they are richly illustrated to facilitate landscape recognition. We begin with Belon's route and its starting point at the village of Kotsinas.

Kotsinas and Phtheleidia Spring: Belon's route

The village of Kotsinas

Kotsinas or Kotzinos is today a tiny coastal village which lies at the northeastern extremity of a zone of pyroclastic volcanic rocks forming a broad area of high ground that extends from Romanou northwards to Varos (Fig. 8). The Byzantine castle at Kotsinas (Fig. 9) dates to the early 12th century and the settlement that grew around it between the 12th and the 15th century served as the second port of the island, following the silting of the bay of Hephaistias (Pennas 1994). It was here that the last emperor of Byzantium, Constantine XI, was forced to disembark with his young pregnant wife on their way to Constantinople in 1442, as they waited for a ferocious storm to

Fig. 9 *Remains of the foundation of the Kotsinas castle.*

33

subside. But Catherine Gatelouzo, whose prestigious family owned the castle, died at childbirth together with her baby who was born prematurely. A modern church (Zoodochos Pigi) has been built within the boundaries of the castle (Fig. 10), and within its courtyard there are 64 subterranean steps leading to a vaulted underground chamber, and into the volcanic rocks that form a broad area of high ground that extends from Romanou northwards to Varos (Fig. 8).

The subterranean vaulted chamber gives access to the waters of a natural spring called *ayiasma* (holy water) (Fig. 11). A chapel with *ayiasma* is clearly noted in Belon's map of Fig. 5, suggesting that, although the castle may have gone into disuse, a small chapel continued to stand there and its holy water was still venerated.

The village of Kotsinas was well known for its potting tradition and indeed there were still (in 2007) remains of several workshops/kilns in various stages of preservations (Fig. 12). Psaropoulou (1986, 235) mentions a potter, Nikolaos Tsoukalas, whose forebears *"made cups from the earth taken from a locality known as Kokalas"*. The name Kokalas was given to an area of Kotsinas already known from 1355 (Tourptsoglou-Stephanidou 1986, 50).

Psaropoulou (1986, 235) continues: *"The earth was called ayiochoma. No one could tell us - not even Nikolaos Tsoukalas - how and why his forebears began making cups especially from ayiochoma. All they knew was that these cups had the property of neutralising any poison placed in them, according to some, or changing the colour of their contents"*. Therefore Tsoukalas' statement made to Psaropoulou in the latter part of the 20th century seems to echo the continuation of a long tradition. On the issue of pottery drinking vessels being made of Lemnian Earth, Gerlach's account of November 1577 tells of the gift that a certain Zygomalas, dignitary of the Patriarchate, brought to his master, the

Fig. 10 *Church of Zoodochos Pigi (right) and Kotsinas harbour.*

Fig. 11 (left) *Steps leading to a subterranean spring (ayiasma) below the modern church at Kotsinas. The underground vaulted chamber must have existed at Belon's time and is reported by him (see Fig. 5).* **Fig. 12 (right)** *Remains of pottery workshop/kiln in Kotsinas.*

ambassador von Ungnad. The gift consisted of *"forty pieces of sealed earth"* and a fine cup made out of the same material that he (Zygomalas) brought from Lemnos (Gerlach in Tourptsoglou-Stephanidou 1986, 110). Gerlach had visited the hillock where Lemnian Earth was extracted. He said that there were three veins: *"from one they extracted the red, from the second the grey and the third the white"* reminiscent of Galen's comment on the different varieties/grades of Lemnian Earth, but also highlighting the differences in its colour.

A second point stemming from Gerlach's accounts is that pottery kilns may well have been present in the vicinity of the place of extraction. Remains of highly fired ceramic materials (fragments of kiln walls) were actually observed by us as surface finds while walking in the vicinity of the chapel and at the bottom of the crag possibly pushed there during ploughing of the adjacent field (Photos-Jones *et al.* 2000).

Just north-west of the bay of Kotsinas, and about 100 m from the shore, potter's clay was located in 1998 in disintegrating plastic bags outside a derelict workshop. A sample was obtained and analysed with XRD. The clay contained minor calcite and trace feldspar which made it similar to soil and rock samples from Kastro Vouni and alluvial sediment from a locality about 500 m SW of Hephaistias. The sample is therefore inferred to represent local clay suitable for the manufacture of pottery and as such provides comparative material for any clay analyses associated with future potential samples of Lemnian Earth.

The area of the Phtheleidia spring

The earliest photograph of the location of the extraction of the Earth is given by Sealy (1919) who marked it with an 'x' (Fig. 13). About 80 years later we took a photograph of the same location (Fig. 14). We were taken to a shallow pit at the top of the ridge (Fig. 15) by a local confident about the 'exact' location of the pit. Given that Lemnian Earth and indeed most earths originated from excavated pits, it was apparent from the start that this location could not be 'disputed'; no specimens of the clay mineral were going to be evident or retrievable from the surface. Thus our search was focused not on finding Lemnian Earth *per se* but rather on pointers to it; thus, the 'site' was simply recorded and photographed.

Fig. 13 (left) *Sealy's (1919) photograph showing site of supposed pit where Lemnian Earth was once extracted on a ridge south east of the chapel of Aghios Sotiras. The cross on the original photograph marks the location of the pit.*
Fig. 14 (right) *View towards the same locality as in Fig. 13 as it appeared in 1998. The landscape looks barely altered.*

Fig. 15 *The pit in the purported locality of extraction of Lemnian Earth, as shown to us in 1998.*

Associated with the shallow pit was a spring. This is presumably the Phtheloudia spring marked as water trough/spring in Fig. 16. The Phthelidia (or sometimes 'Phthelouda') spring is located in the greater Kotsinas area and is presently inelegantly rebuilt in cement and brick and with a trough for watering animals (Fig. 18). The small chapel of Aghios Sotiras (St Saviour) lies to the east. In 1998 the chapel stood in splendid isolation against the backdrop of the crags (Fig. 20) in a landscape not dissimilar to that observed by Sealy at the turn of the 20th century. However in 2007 there were two additional buildings erected to the north of it which were, at the time, at varying stages of completion (Fig. 19). There was a two-storey private house and a new built church of considerable proportions. Presently, there may be additional structures/features in the landscape. The spring is accessed via a track/path (Figs. 16 and 19) from the main road.

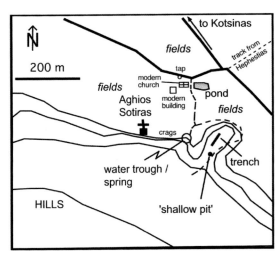

Fig. 16 *The area in the immediate vicinity of the Phtheleidia spring, highlighting key features within. This is the inset shown in Fig. 8.*

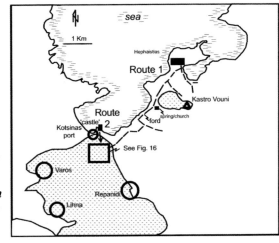

Fig. 17 *Map of the two paths taken by Galen (Route 1) and Belon (Route 2) to arrive at the same locality of extraction of the Lemnian Earth, namely the area of the Phtheleidia spring (see Fig. 16).*

37

Fig. 18 *Long trough in front of Phtheleidia spring; water is piped from the spring to the trough.*

As shown in Fig. 16, the track splits before reaching the spring/trough, with a branch extending westwards and upwards curving round to the north. It is also possible to walk eastwards along the base of the crags to the small chapel of Aghios Sotiras but there is no distinct pathway. There is a modern tap situated on the main paved road which may be fed by the Phtheleidia spring by pipe, as well as an overgrown depression to the west of the track. At the time of our visit it was surrounded by masonry debris and covered by a thick growth of fig trees. It is marked in Fig.16 as 'pond'.

When Belon (1588) visited the site of the spring, he set off from the castle of Kotsinas (Fig. 17, route 2) already in ruins. His measurement of distances in terms of 'arrow-shots' make it difficult to follow, nevertheless, given that the distances involved are not large, we could retrace his steps: *"From the corner of the castle (Kotsinas) towards the left, we walked towards the hill which is not more than four arrow-shots away. Between the port and the hill there is a small chapel called St Saviour's, where the monks gather on the 6th of August, the date set for the extraction of the earth from its vein. After leaving the chapel and walking towards the hillock we found two paths, one to the left and one to the right leading to two springs, one about one arrow-shot away from the other"*. Later on he adds, *"they (priests and monks) walk towards and climb the hill which is not more than two arrow-shots away from the chapel"* (Belon in Tourptsoglou-Stephanidou 1986). The passage from Belon suggests that he approached the spring from the east, ie the chapel of St Saviour, probably by walking through what is today a field under cultivation. Belon continues, *"the one on our right (the Phthelidia) does not dry up in the summer, however, the one on the left does so completely...with horses we continued towards the right, towards a place where no trees grow, except of a carob tree, ... and a willow which shadow the spring and where there are stone steps so that one can access the place where they extract the "sealed earth". One climbs uphill and further up towards one's left one can see the place where they extract the earth on the*

Fig. 19 *Modern buildings and chapel with view of track leading from main road to spring. View towards SSE. The group of fig trees that mark a boggy depression can be seen to left of the modern church. St Saviour (Aghios Sotiras) can be seen in the background to right with lush pine tree. Photo taken in 2007.*

6th of August. Because they extract it after opening a vein, nothing other than a long trench covered with earth can be seen".

On noting Belon's reference to two springs, it is important to read into it the notion of a pond or stream rather than water issuing from the subsurface. The fact that one of the two dried up in the summer suggests that one was indeed a pond and this is highlighted as such in Fig. 16. Belon's reference to a long trench is intriguing since we indeed came across a long trench (Fig. 21) which was *c.* 5 m long and about 30 cm wide, up-hill and to the east of the Phthelidia spring. The trench is cut into volcanic rock (Fig. 22) and is therefore likely to be long-lasting. However, we think it could well have been opened, or re-opened, by the Greek army because there was a disused camouflaged observation post just below. Dioscorides (*Material Medica* Book V.113) mentions that the Earth came out of '*a certain hollow cavern having a marshy place*', alluding if not to a trench certainly a cavern -like feature. Belon's description of the spring's location corresponds to the area of the Phthelidia spring.

Fig. 20 *Chapel of St Saviour (Aghios Sotiras) and view looking north towards Kotsinas bay. The picture illustrates the very subdued topography of the route taken by Belon from Kotsinas to the Phtheleidia Spring.*

39

Fig. 21 *View to NE of the 'trench' above Phthelidia spring. It is unlikely that this trench is of some antiquity, yet the fact that Belon refers to a similar feature in the same locality is of interest. The trench is reproduced here in black and white to better illustrate the feature.*

This part of the island, a coastal plain, is now more intensely cultivated than would have been the case at the time of Belon's visit, and there are several modern roads cutting across the route.

When walking southwards up the path (Fig. 19) we noticed reddish and yellowish stones used as fill in places. These are the most altered rocks in the area and provide evidence of local hydrothermal alteration that could well relate to the origin of Lemnian Earth. Further clues are likely to be under the fields closer to the spring and the crags, the exposed rock at the bottom of the hill. There is no outcrop of clay bed fitting the description of Lemnian Earth to be seen in the vicinity, corroborating the observation that Lemnian Earth existed at 'depth' and would only be recovered by digging.

While Belon started his journey at Kotsinas, Galen started his from Hephaistias (Fig. 17, route 1). In order to retrace Galen's route to the area of extraction of the Lemnian Earth, i.e. the area of the Phtheleidia spring, it is important to start from the Hephaistias car park and follow the coastal route in the opposite direction to the archaeological site, as described in the pages that follow. It takes about three hours of leisurely walking to complete Galen's route.

Fig. 22 *View to NW from the 'trench' above the Phthelidia Spring and towards the modern church; also shown is the path (highlighted in purple) leading from the main road (grey) to the spring. The rock outcrop in the foreground is the type of rock out of which the spring water emerges. The area circled in grey shows the location of the 'pond'.*

Hephaistias and Kastro Vouni: Galen's route

Hephaistias

The cross-country and, in 2007, still un-surfaced track from the main road to Hephaistias takes us generally northwards close to the north-western end of the ridge of Kastro Vouni before running downhill and past the end of the bay to the car park for the site. The site of Hephaistias (Fig. 23) which requires several hours to visit occupies a hilly peninsula in the north of the island (Fig. 8) and extends north from the present car parking area. The inland bay is clearly being gradually filled with silt, yet it is likely that Galen sailed from the open sea (Fig. 2) into the security of this bay (Fig. 6). Walking to the shore one can see stonework representing the remains of the harbour (Fig. 24).

Between 1926 and 1931 the Italian School of Archaeology conducted excavations at Hephaistias, under the direction of Professor Della Seta, in the areas of the cemetery and the town with dated remains from Archaic to Hellenistic and later periods. In 1929-30, a small ceremonial building was revealed, the *sacello*, together with some Hellenistic structures (later identified as kilns for the production of "*coppe megaresi*" (Megarian bowls)), at the southern end of the *hieron* which was discovered in 1979.

Fig. 23 *View of Hephaistias looking north towards the area of the theatre.*

41

In the 1970s a new survey took place and in 1978 a trench was cut, starting from the *sacello* and linking the two areas of excavation of the 1929-1930 season. The discovery of an *hieron* corroborated the original suggestion that during the 7th century BC the entire area may have been a ceremonial complex, the little building (*sacello*) serving as the *adyton* (Di Vita 1986, 442-491). The *adyton* was the most restricted to access part of the temple where the image of the god was kept. The *sacello* was accessed through a long room (oriented in a northeast-southwest direction), which was probably roofless, with an entrance from the southwest, through a narrow *pronaos*, and with a floor made of compacted red earth. Measuring 2.80 x 3 m, it had a door on the south-eastern side and a large tank in the north-western side held in place by a large poros slab. Its walls were also made of large and small blocks of poros stone. A pithos and ritual objects (including a Y-shaped cylindrical clay figurine) were found within the *sacello* or occupied the empty space in front of the tank; numerous other objects were found inside the tank, indicating that the *sacello* constituted a sort of *adyton* to the *hieron*, with the two cylinders at its end containing the remains or ritual functions (animal bones, vessels for libations, and bird figurines). Although the *hieron* belongs to the end of the 7th century BC (the end of the local sub-Geometric period), the *sacello* instead bore resemblance to similar constructions dating to the Minoan period (*sacello* at Knossos) and to similar ones of later date (sanctuary of Kaviri at Samothrace, and the Telesterion at Eleusis). The *hieron* seems to be associated with the cults and religion of the Tyrrhenians, who worshipped the Great Goddess of Nature. The floor was covered by a *c.* 20 cm thick layer of 'terra rossa battuta' (translated from the Italian as compressed red earth), lying over a stratum of broken rocks, covering the rocky natural ground (Messineo 1993, 417). In the course of the 1981 excavations further features were revealed (Di Vita 1988

Fig. 24 *View over the silted-up harbour in Hephaistias Bay, towards the NE. Galen would have sailed into the bay through the straits in the distance.*

201-208). Two parallel water channels *'canalette litiche'* of rectangular section (*c.* 5 cm per side) were deeply cut into the rocky floor and ran slightly obliquely to the longitudinal axis of the *hieron*. The first channel started from the *poros* walls of the *sacello*, and had three outlets for overflow. The second channel started from the *hieron*. Establishing a function for the channels has been problematic for the excavators. Indeed, there is no attempt to relate these features in any way to activities related to Lemnian Earth. It is possible that the function of the channels consisted of protecting the fired compacted floor from the water flow out of the *sacello*, however whether its function was practical or ritual was difficult for the excavators to ascertain. In the intervening centuries the *sacello*, partly destroyed and possibly intentionally protected under a layer of earth (Messineo 1993, 425), was eventually built over.

Patches of red earth can be seen clearly today at the entrance to the sanctuary, presumably the remains of *'terra rossa battuta'* (Fig. 25). In a landscape devoid of red colour, these red patches certainly stand out. But it remains to be seen whether that red earth is actually related to the grey Kotsinas pottery clay or perhaps to the processing of Lemnian Earth. At the time of our visit there we did not have permission to sample, however sampling of this *terra rossa battuta* in the future would be worthwhile to confirm this hypothesis. Nevertheless, it is noted that these potentially parallel activities - pottery manufacture and Lemnian Earth processing - may have been taking place much earlier than the time of Galen; the memory of them lived on and the practice may have been revived at least on a larger scale in the Ottoman period.

Fig. 25 *'Terra rossa battuta' in the foreground of the image and at the entry to the sanctuary. In the background and under cover can be discerned the sacello. Patches of red earth are exceedingly rare in the Hephaistias area.*

Kastro Vouni

In the greater Hephaistias area one particular locality stuck out as a candidate for exploration, the hillock of Kastro Vouni. Sealy mentioned it in his account of places to visit on Lemnos on the basis that it was the mythical hill Mosychlos, *"the hill to which at the time I (Galen) disembarked, the priestess came"*. Galen adds that the sacred hill was in the territory of the town called Hephaistias (Galen *On Simple Drugs* IX.II.247-8; Brock 1929, 193). There exists no toponym, Mosychlos, on any of the known maps, only in legend and as a result of the 19th century revival of the word (Phil. Bouttman 1807 in Tourptsoglou-Stephanidou 1986, 562). On Belon's map (Fig. 5) it is represented as *Mons Vulcani unde terra lemnia effoditur* (the mountain of Vulcan where they extract Lemnian Earth). Kastro Vouni is not a volcano but does resemble one (Fig. 26) and the profile of the range is very similar to the range drawn in Belon's map (Fig. 5).

Fig. 26 *Kastro Vouni (peak on extreme left of image) viewed from the Hephaistias archaeological site.*

Sealy (1919, 167) reported and photographed the presence of an underground feature (Fig. 27) at the summit of Kastro Vouni, investigated at the end of the 19th century by De Launay (De Launay in Tourptsoglou-Stephanidou 1986, 498) and drawn in section by him; we were able to photograph part of this feature through an opening and by suspending a camera from the surface (Fig. 28). De Launay (in Tourptsoglou-Stephanidou 1986, 497) wrote that *"after a bit of ....gymnastics, admittedly rather easy, I managed to get through a hole ...and I found myself in a sort of underground room, which come to think of it, must be the ruins of an old byzantine chapel"*. Local oral tradition refers to the discovery of a marble statue of a reclining female body found sometime in the latter part of the 19th century. This feature was thought, De Launay reports, to have been associated with yet another myth relating to Lemnos, the Labyrinth of Lemnos, one of the four labyrinths known in the ancient world. The other three labyrinths were located at Knossos in Crete, in Egypt and in Italy (Etruria) and are mentioned by Pliny (*Nat. Hist.* XXXVI.90). The Lemnian one was famous for its 150 columns and apparently movable (revolving?) doors that could be opened with a mere child's push. To our knowledge no proper archaeological survey has been carried out on the summit of Kastro Vouni and on the feature itself so any connection between the underground chamber (perhaps a cistern?) at the top of KastroVouni and the 'Lemnian Labyrinth' will require further investigation. The mortared wall surface of the feature suggests a late date of construction.

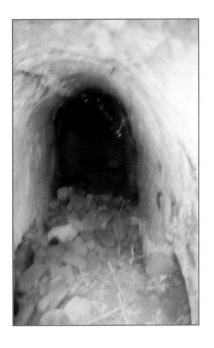

Fig. 27 (above) *Kastro Vouni: photo of interior of the feature at summit taken by Sealy (1919, 167).* **Fig. 28 (right)** *Kastro Vouni: view of part of the same feature, at the time of our first visit in 1998.*

It is concluded that the greater Hephaistias area is not a likely candidate for the presence of Lemnian Earth, with the exception of the *hieron* itself to which it was perhaps transported. In reference to the Kastro Vouni, possibly the hill on which Hephaistos was purported to have fallen, this is almost certainly not the hill of its extraction at least from a geological viewpoint explained below. However, a more detailed survey, both geochemical and geophysical, particularly geared towards the elucidation of the purported features at the top of Kastro Vouni might bring to light additional information regarding Lemnian Earth and perhaps the myth of the Lemnian Labyrinth.

The rocks of this region are well exposed both along the coast and on hillsides inland and consist of bedded sedimentary rocks (Fig. 29). These were examined, sampled and analysed with the possibility of beds of montmorillonite-bearing mudstones in mind as these might be potential Lemnian Earth. Fine grey mudstone, possibly tuffaceous, and representing what is probably the most abundant sedimentary rock (the Eocene/Oligocene sequence) in the vicinity of Hephaistias was sampled on the lower eastern slopes of Kastro Vouni. The mudstone is slightly weathered and in places, as a result of more extreme weathering, has developed a distinct yellow-brown colour, which is typical of the local soil formed over the Eocene/Oligocene sedimentary rocks. Layers of harder rock, possibly sandstone or indurated tuff, up to 1m thick were noted in this area. Although the mudstone was relatively soft, it did not become 'slimy' on moistening as would have been expected for mudstone rich in expanding smectitic clays. Indeed, the clay minerals in samples recovered and analysed by XRD did not contain significant amounts of expanding clay. Also, there was no evidence that any special 'earths', rich in expanding clays, kaolin and/or aluminous sulphates for example, were likely to be found on the top of this hill or in the vicinity, and this was supported by XRD analysis of soil from the summit. In conclusion, no sites with potential for 'special clays', were observed on or near Kastro Vouni.

Fig. 29 *Bedded rocks by road-side near Kastro Vouni.*

Galen's route

During his visit to Hephaistias, Galen was clearly alerted to his surroundings:
"....as to what the poet said about Hephaistos, that he fell in Lemnos, it seems to me that the fable refers to the nature of the hill, which has every appearance of having been burned, both on account of its colour, and from the fact that nothing grows on it. This then was the hill to which at the time I disembarked the priestess came" (Galen *On Simple Drugs* IX.II.247-8; Brock 1929, 193).

In reference to the colour of the Earth, he further adds *"......it is also like the hill of Lemnos, which is entirely tawny in colour, and on which there is neither tree nor rock nor plant, but only this kind of earth"* (*On Simple Drugs* IX.II.247-8; Brock 1929, 192). It seems unlikely that the colour of the hills has anything to do with the colour of Lemnian Earth; finer-grained material and a lump of the same material can have different colours.

In order to retrace the route that Galen took following the procession of the priestess (see Fig. 30f which gives the location of each photograph 30a-e, along that route), we recommend that one drives to the car park at the entrance to the archaeological site of Hephaistias. Then take the track that is inland from the coast and runs west from the Hephaistias car park area, past a farmyard. The view back towards Hephaistias and the bay can be seen in Figure 30a.

There are several places where tracks split (e.g. Fig. 30b and marked as (b) in the path), but the main track continues following generally the east coast. One of the branches on the track (Figs. 30b and 30f) leads south along the foot of the Kastro Vouni ridge. Continuing along the track the local bedrock can be seen below light-coloured soils on the south side of the track where it has been cut into the field.

Leaving the car park the track follows the contours around the Kastro Vouni ridge and soon a spring is found with a small church nearby (Figs. 30c and 30d marked as (c) and (d) in Fig 30f). There is no evidence in the vicinity of this spring and church that would indicate that it could be a potential site for Lemnian Earth. For example, the local soils/sediments are pale brown and there is no indication of volcanic activity or hydrothermal alteration. The track continues downhill to a ford then uphill (see Fig. 30f). Take the turning to the right near the top of the hill to continue towards the

Phtheledia spring area. If instead of going right one continues to the left it is possible to arrive at the abandoned Turkish village Aghia Hypate, mentioned in many travellers accounts as the place of the washing of the Earth. The old traditional buildings there are now mainly in a ruinous state (Fig. 30e and marked as (e) in Fig 30f). The coastal track leads eventually to Kotsinas. Walk through the village of Kotsinas and reach the road going towards Rapinidi. One crosses that road and takes the path leading to the Phthelidia spring area.

Fig. 30a *View NE along track to Hephaistias harbour.*

Fig. 30b *Looking NE along track to Hephaistias bay. The track to the right goes towards Kastro Vouni.*

Fig. 30e *Ruinous building in village of Ayia Ypate.*

Fig. 30c *View to NE. Small church with spring by the track. The track continues downhill to a ford then uphill (see Fig. 30f). Take the turning to the right near the top of the hill to continue towards the Phtheleidia spring area.*

Fig. 30d *Spring with Ottoman style carving along the track. There is a gently rising narrow path leading to the chapel.*

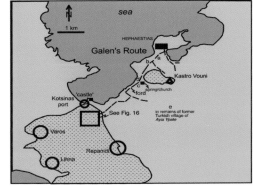

Fig. 30f *Key locations mentioned in the text and illustrated in the photos on these pages.*

Geological background to Lemnos

Lemnos is dominated by young Cenozoic (Upper Eocene to Lower Oligocene) sedimentary rocks which consist of both marine and terrestrial sediments (Fig. 31). These include 'sandy' beds (conglomerates, sandstones, siltstones), carbonates (marls and limestone) as well as some tuffaceous volcanics (Fig. 31). Such sedimentary rocks underlie the topographically gentle areas in the northern-central, north-eastern and extreme southern parts of the island. Younger Lower Miocene volcanic rocks, both lavas and pyroclastics, outcrop in a general east-west zone through the central area of the island. These rocks, being more resistant to weathering, are responsible for and underlie the more hilly and rugged areas of the island. The youngest sedimentary rocks (of Pleistocene age) are calcareous sandstones that form very minor deposits at a few localities around the periphery of the island. Holocene alluvial sediments occupy extensive low ground in the centre and the east of the island. A significant concentration of intrusive rocks of calc-alkali mafic to felsic composition occur in sediments in the extreme southern and north-western parts of the island, but from their distribution on the geological map these do not appear to relate to well-defined magmatic centres. However, the notable development of andesitic to felsic lavas in the western part of the island attests to the presence of a volcanic centre. The presence of silicified trees in the pyroclastic formations (tuffs) in the centre-east area provides evidence of a terrestrial environment of volcanism followed by hydrothermal alteration that resulted in silicification. As well as the hydrothermally altered igneous rocks, there are two extensive zones of altered sedimentary rocks located in the southern half of the island. The alteration is described on IGME's (1993) geological map of Lemnos as impregnations of iron and sulphur minerals. This provides evidence of the potential for unrecorded hydrothermal mineral occurrences and more substantial hydrothermal mineralisation at depth.

In summary, there are no metamorphic basement rocks exposed as is typical of Aegean islands, but rather a sequence of sedimentary rocks which initially formed in a relatively deep water marine environment indicated by turbidites (sediments typically deposited rapidly from submarine mudflows) and channels with conglomerates. Gradually the environment became less marine and eventually terrestrial as volcanic products increased. Geological faulting with a general E-W trend and minor folding, again with an E-W trend of fold axes, most evident in the bedded sedimentary sequence are indicative of tectonism that presumably took place on uplift of the island relative to sea level. And this was followed by erosion to give the present form and topography of the island. It is worth emphasising, in view of the frequent references to

Lemnos being a volcanic island, that volcanic activity on Lemnos is very ancient and was long extinct before human occupation of the island. We can only infer from this that the Hephaistos myth was re-iterating events reminiscent of volcanic activity. From the above it is deduced that the geological setting and geological history of the island indicates that there is potential for sulphur-bearing hydrothermal mineralisation and therefore acid sulphate alteration related to volcanism. It is hydrothermal alteration of this style that has the potential to produce both red (iron oxide) and yellow/white (clay - kaolin) products. Also there is the potential for deposits of the expanding clay, montmorillonite, to form as a result of alteration of feldspathic volcanic rocks.

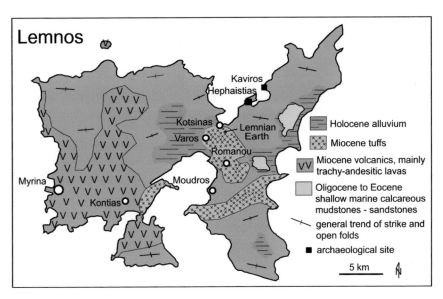

Fig. 31 *Simplified geological map of Lemnos (after IGME 1993).*

A back-filled 'pit' in alluvial sediments, SW of Hephaistias

During our fruitless search for red soils and sediments in the geological out-crops in the area around Hephaistias, we noticed small reddish vertical 'streaks' in the sub-soil of a trackside-cutting about 500 m southwest of the entrance to the archaeological site of Hephaistias. This back-filled 'pit' is briefly described below (see Figs. 32a and 32b). Small reddish vertical 'streaks' were noted in the sub-soil of a trackside-cutting about 500 m south-west of the entrance to the archaeological site of Hephaistias. Here alluvial sediments unconformably overlie weathered beds of north-east-dipping Eo-cene/Oligocene calcareous siltstones. The reddish zones appeared as two parallel vertical strips, 1-20 mm wide, about 1.5 m long and about 1.5 m apart. On closer examination, the reddish strips could be seen to clearly mark the sides of an infilled cavity, potentially a natural gully or a man-made trench or pit, which extended down almost to bedrock. The infill con-sists of sandy sediment containing some pebbles and a few shells of land snails. The bottom of the feature was marked by a thin (1-20 mm) layer of black carbonaceous sediment. The three-dimensional shape of the original feature remains unknown as this could not be determined in the field with-out excavation but a pit-shape is most likely.

Since this appeared to be the only locality with a red colour in the vicinity of Hephaistias it was decided to sample and examine the nature of this col-oration. The geological samples collected included: the brown friable weathered calcareous bedrock about 3 m SW of the pit feature; pale brown weathered bedrock immediately SW of the pit; pale brown pebbly alluvium from within the pit; the fine red sediment (a few cm thick) that marked the right (SW) side of the pit. and the black carbonaceous sediment (about 2 cm thick) that marked the base of the pit. The reddish coloration is clearly due to reddening of the local sediment on the edge of the original cavity/pit; small brownish pebbles had, for example, been reddened on one side. There was no indication that the cavity/pit had been lined with a coating of red clay. The poorly consolidated nature of the sediments which would be unstable in a near vertical section, suggests that the cavity was indeed a pit which was dug and then backfilled after a short time interval. A provisional conclusion was made in the field that there had been a fire in the pit and the steep walls had been reddened by the heat. The feature described here was visible in 1998 in the course of our first visit to Lemnos. There were no traces of that feature visible in 2007.

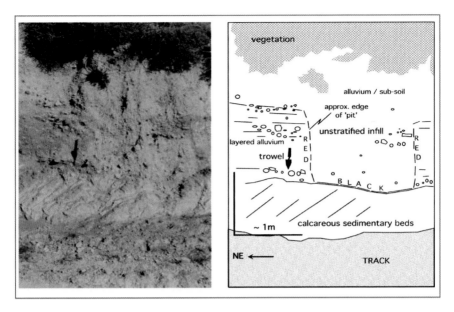

Fig. 32a *(left)* *View of the 'back-filled pit'. Note the thin red streaks marking the sides of the former cavity and the black layer at the base.* **Fig. 32b** *(right)* *Sketch showing details of 'back-filled pit' as seen on left.*

The geology of the Phthelidia spring area

On the hill of *ayiochoma*, where the pit shown in Fig. 16 is located, and immediately south of the Phthelidia spring, there are light-yellow to yellow slightly altered pyroclastic volcanic rocks of biotite-hornblende dacitic-andesite composition. Within light-coloured surface material are rare relicts of fresh volcanic rock and isolated feldspar phenocrysts. Samples of this rock, although not *in situ*, were collected and x-ray diffraction analyses indicate that the clay mineral montmorillonite/illite is the main component. This represents an alteration product of weathered and/or hydrothermally altered feldspars and volcanic glass. There are also cristobalite, relict feldspar, quartz and alunite present. Alunite and montmorillonite are of special significance to understanding the potential nature of Lemnian Earth. Alunite has the formula $KAl_3(SO_4)_2(OH)_6$. and it is relatively insoluble. Alum is the general name for a group of minerals which are soluble aluminum-rich sulphates.

The concentration of alunite is not the same in all collected samples and it is always less than montmorillonite/illite. Samples collected from near the

53

spring and from the nearby trench have variable colour. They are brown to brownish yellow or red with white parts. Petrographic (Fig. 33) and XRD analyses indicate that the white parts consist of alunite as the main component with kaolinite and cristobalite, whereas the red ochreous matrix contains alunite and kaolinite with hematite, goethite, amorphous iron oxyhydroxides and quartz. Feldspar occurs as relict idiomorphic crystals rimmed with alunite which also forms micro-veinlets. The cristobalite replaces primary feldspars, whereas kaolin, quartz and iron oxyhydroxides form a very fine reddish matrix. These samples thus show pronounced alteration, presumably hydrothermal, which is not unexpected in the proximity of a geological fault in a former volcanic area. This fault apparently crossed the site of the present-day spring and this site presumably also constituted the main focus for the hydrothermal solutions.

Boulders and smaller fragments of altered volcanic rocks were also observed in the track leading to the spring. They consisted of fragments of red and white altered volcanic rock; the presence of sulphur, consistent with the presence of alunite, was confirmed by qualitative SEM-EDAX analysis. Fine silt (accumulating near the edge of the track proved on XRD analysis to be rich in expanding clay further confirming the presence of montmorillonite-type expanding (absorbing) clays in this area. We therefore infer that the different 'varieties' of earths with various textures (sticky, greasy and granular) and colours (white, yellow and red) which are referred to in various texts are products of the same hydrothermal alteration with various proportions of the alteration products (Photos-Jones *et al.* 2000).

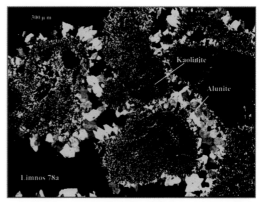

Fig. 33 *Photomicrograph of thin section (transmitted light, crossed-polars) showing alunite in altered volcanic rock. The polycrystalline alunite rims kaolin-rich cores, presumably all a product of the hydrothermal alteration of feldspar (image taken by V. Perdikatsis, then at the Institute of Geological and Mining Exploration).*

Alum and astringency

No discussion on astringent earths can be undertaken without tackling the issue of alum, the most potent of astringent compounds. Theophrastus does not mention alum in his treatise *On Stones* but Pliny (Eichholz 1965) refers to a missing book by Theophrastus *On Salt, Nitre, and Alum*. Alum had many functions: as an emetic when mixed with copper (*Nat. Hist.* XXXIV.106), for eye complaints, as a panacea pill, with salt or soda and vinegar for sores, leprosy and ulcers, finishing textiles and skins, dyes (the mordant to fix the dye), for gilding copper (*Nat. Hist.* XXXIII.65), as a solder (*Nat. Hist.* XXXIII.88), for cleaning gold (*Nat. Hist.* XXXV.183) and also as a flame retardant (Claudius *Quadrigarius*, fr. 81).

Galen recognized the astringency of Lemnian Earth: "τούτων δ'απασών η Λημνία δύναμιν ισχυροτέραν έχει, προσέστι γαρ αυτή τι και στύψεως" (of all the above (earths), Lemnian Earth is the most potent, because in it there is a bit of alum) (*On simple Drugs* XIII.252; author's (EPJ) translation).

'Alum' is a mineral group name. The alum group consists of a large number of very soluble hydrated sulphates (usually aluminium-rich sulphates), such as alunogen, $Al_2(SO_4)_3.17H_2O$, and potassium-alum (K-alum), $KAl(SO_4)_2.12H_2O$. We therefore use the name 'alum' here for alum that is dominantly aluminium sulphate hydrate with or without potassium. Alum was still of such commercial importance (as a mordant) in the early 20th century that alum nomenclature was the subject of a book where it was argued that the word alum should be used only for potassium alum (Richardson 1927). The main concern seemed to be that K-alum was the standard material in use at that time, and its commercial status was being undermined by calling other minerals alum, in particular alunogen. Alum has long been known for its astringency or styptic/haemostatic property. The word 'astringency' implies a 'drawing together', 'shrinkage' and 'drying' of soft body tissues as well as a 'sharp' taste sensation. Astringency, in the former sense, is a significant property of alum in relation to its medicinal and pharmaceutical uses.

Aluminium is soluble in acidic solutions and when alum is dissolved in water, the resulting solution is quite acidic. The aluminium is likely to be in the form of the relatively small and relatively highly charged cation, Al^{+++}, although it may also be present in the form of dissolved aluminium species - more complex large cations that have negatively charged groups attached to the cation. It is the relatively high positive charge on the small cation that gives Al^{+++} its special chemical properties and has meant that in most geochemical environments it has never been readily available to become a component in a beneficial or even a harmful biochemical molecule, in normal life-processes. It is now regarded as being toxic to humans but is of relatively minor concern as there are few routes for it to enter the human biochemical system. One significant concern has been its possible role in Alzheimer's disease, the suggestion being that even very low concentrations of aluminium can proceed through the human body to cause damage to brain function. We consider (in July 2011) that there is a need for more biochemical research on aluminium in order to understand its astringent and antibacterial properties, and this should help underpin our understanding of the medicinal use of alum in antiquity.

What is astringency? Astringency is generally considered to be the property, displayed by a group of substances, of shrinking mucous membranes and drying up secretions. Astringents are now classified by their mode of action into:
(a) those that decrease the blood supply by narrowing the blood vessels;
(b) those that remove water;
(c) those that coagulate superficial layers into a crust.

Astringents known as styptics are employed to dry up excessive secretions and to stop oozing of blood. We usually use the word 'astringency' following (c). However, astringency is also used to refer to a taste sensation (Lawless *et al*. 1994), the reason for the taste impact relating to the biochemical properties of astringents which are listed above. It seems to us, therefore, that the 'taste' aspect of 'astringency' is not as 'fundamental' as the three biochemical impacts listed above, but it is understandable that the word 'astringent' has become associated with the 'quality of taste' of fruit for example (Lawless *et al*. 1994; Eaks 1967). Tannic acids have been recognised as a reason for fruit astringency (Eaks 1967) and a test for tannic acids has been devised that involves using ferric chloride to precipitate and assess the amount of tannic acids in a fruit. This is reminiscent of Pliny's account of the use of pomegranate juice to assess the purity of alum (Pliny *Nat Hist* XXXV.184). Iron, as an impurity in alum, would have deleterious effects with certain organic dyes. We have assessed this test and considered it to be a sensitive one for the presence of iron impurity in alum, even when the concentration of iron is as little as a few hundred ppm. (Hall and Photos-Jones 2009). It is most likely that it is the chemical properties of aluminium, in the form of alum or just as the chemical, aluminium sulphate within clay, that are the reason for, or at least a major contributor to, the medicinal benefits of the earths. There is a second significant property of alum to consider in addition to astringency and that is antibacterial activity.

Antibacterial activity of alum

Although alum is widely acclaimed to be a natural deodorant that works because of its antibacterial properties, we have found (to July 2011) no systematic studies in the scientific literature that explain such antibacterial activity. Nevertheless, there are good indications that alum, presumably the dissolved aluminium, does indeed behave as a bactericide, for example, clinical research on its use as a mouth rinse (Mourughan and Suryakanth 2004), although any bactericidal properties of alum appear to be refuted by some researchers (Taj and Baquai 2007). Our research has suggested that it is alum in Lemnian Earth that is the active ingredient as a bactericide and perhaps to a lesser extent the montmorillonite clay itself (see section below: a recipe for Lemnian Earth).

Samian Earth

Samos is a large island situated in the Eastern Aegean close to the Turkish border. It is mountainous with extensive forested areas over 600 m high (Figs. 1a and 1b). The timber used in shipping contributed to Samos being a rich and powerful city state in Archaic and Classical Greece (Shipley 1987, 12). There are however also extensive lowlands suitable for arable crops. Shipley (1987, 233-238) gives the distribution of archaeological sites of all periods, although he notes the sparsity of prehistoric sites. The main sites include the Heraion and the Pythagoreion, the latter comprising the tunnel of Eupalinos, first reported by Herodotus (*Histories* 3.60); it was built in the 6th century BC under the tyrant Polycrates, a remarkable feat of engineering for supplying water from an inland spring to the coastal town of ancient Samos. The Heraion, which was a sanctuary dedicated to Hera, has large temples whose foundations go back to the Geometric period (Shipley 1987, 78; Kyrieleis 1981).

Theophrastus mentioned that, although Samian Earth was 'beautiful', it was 'greasy' and unlike Melian Earth, implying that it was unsuitable for painting; rather he noted that "*the Earth is used mainly, if not entirely, for treating cloaks*" (*On Stones* 62-4). The white variety was the best known. He also stated that the Samian miners had to work by lying on their sides with rocks above and below in workings about 2 feet high. Dioscorides (*De Materia Medica* V.172) wrote that Samian Earth is extremely white and light in weight and *"in touching the tongue holds it fast like glue'*; the substance is called κολλύριον, this word corresponding to 'eye-salve'. The second variety is called 'aster' *'being crusty and thick like whetstone'*. Samian Earth resembles Eretrian Earth in its use for burnishing and washing.

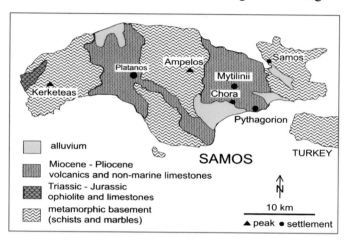

Fig. 34 *Simplified geological map of Samos showing place names mentioned in the text.*

In addition to Samian Earth, Dioscorides (*De Materia Medica* V.173) mentions *Lithos Samios* (Stone of Samos) which was used to burnish gold, the best one being the white and sturdy one (στιβαρός). It also had medicinal applications. Pliny (*Nat. Hist.* XXXV.191) also identifies two types of Samian Earth: one type called '*colyrium*', an eye salve, and another called '*Aster*' used for the cleaning of cloth. He refers (*Nat. Hist.* XXXVI.152) to *Lapis Samius* or Samian Stone as distinct from Samian Earth, perhaps because he simply followed Dioscorides' statement. There are also two types of stone: the first is soft and sticks to the tongue, and the second is more dense. Pliny (*Nat. Hist.* XXXV.16 and XXXVI.21) reiterates the fact that there are two types of Samian Earth and lists the medicinal applications: good for αιμόπτυσιν (spitting of blood), useful to put on a plaster or salve and good for eye-salves or smearing substances; doctors use it for pains and ulcers in the eye, stomach diseases, epilepsy, diarrhea and urine retention. He also adds that Samian Earth is good for the shining of gold.

Galen, like Pliny, mentions the term αστήρ (IX.4), saying that Samian Earth can be applied to the face and body as if it was some kind of soap (*cf.* Κιμωλία) instead of νίτρον (carbonate of soda) in the baths (Galen *On Simple Drugs* IX.1; XII.181). In his *Περι Ευποριστων* (II.7; 103; 152) he says that it speeds up fever when drunk with various substances. It is good for

58

diarrhea when drunk with water. In the 19th century, Samian Earth was reported to be used in the making of clay vessels (Kritikidis 1869).

Given its proximity to Western Anatolia, Samos shares many of its geological features. There is a metamorphic basement with quartzites, schists and marbles which is overlain by younger Miocene-Pliocene volcanic rocks and non-marine limestones (Fig. 34) in extensive basins. These basins are calcareous lacustrine sedimentary deposits interbedded with siliceous volcanic tuffs and contain evaporite minerals such as potassium and sodium chlorite and niter, sodium nitrate as well as boron enrichments (Stamatakis *et al.* 1989). In the Chora area in a road cutting where the road leaves Chora, there are good exposures of the lower part of interbedded tuffs and limestones with layers of chalcedony.

Further south, the platy limestone has been quarried for use as a building stone and in ancient times was mined underground. Bitumen was observed as dry resinous black coatings in places on the walls of the old mines. It has evidently seeped out of fractures and layers at various times. The seepages seem to be of different ages, coming out of certain layers. There are also chalcedony layers in the limestone and some encrustation/efflorescence on platy limestone. These represent precipitation of soluble salts and were tentatively considered to be nitrates or sulphates in the field. The old mines were very dry, but it is likely that water penetrates downwards into the mines in the wet season, transporting the salts from the overlying layers of rock into the mine. The efflorescences therefore are potential renewable resource of soluble industrial minerals and were sampled to ascertain their identity. The small samples collected proved to be unusual 'wiry' forms of common salt, NaCl.

Guide to localities of Samian Earth

Although the properties and uses of Samian Earth are well documented, the locality of its extraction is less so. There are bentonite clay pits in Samos, within an area of volcanic rock near the village of Platanos (Figs. 34 and 35). It seems unlikely that the original small pits mentioned in Theophrastus would have survived for long, and it is probable that generations of pits were produced in the area over time as the deposits were exploited. The material used for Samian Earth would have come from distinct layers rather than 'seams in a vein' as interpreted by Eichholz (1965, 130-1). The pits would have been excavated down to a layer which thereafter would have been followed laterally for short distances as was the case in the earliest coal-mining bell pits. So the initial excavation of the pit would have produced much waste which, even if located archaeologically, would probably do little to inform us of the material actually being exploited from the pit. Regarding the eye salve, only one material could be considered a relevant candidate and that is a borate such as borax. Borate deposits are rare in the world and appear to result from evaporation of boron-rich lakes in volcanic settings. There is a major deposit at Boron, California in the Mojave desert (Harben and Bates 1990). On Samos, borates occur in the central part of the Miocene Karlovasi basin in the west of Samos (Fig. 34) and have been described in several publications (Stamatakis & Economou 1991; Stamatakis *et al*. 2009). IGME has located borate localities about 3 km west of Platanos including roadside outcrops of calcareous beds which contain coarse white crystals in veins in places, some being borates, some gypsum and some calcium carbonates.

There is an area of pyroclastic rocks including 'saponitic' clays marked on the IGME geological map (Theodoropoulos 1979) near Platanos, and this is the most likely locality for the *aster* variety of Samian Earth that was used as fuller's earth. Also, an 'earth' was found nearby in modern times in quite deep diggings (Bürchner 1892, 41-2) and included off-white fuller's earth. The disused modern workings, as described to Shipley (1987, 277) by local residents at Platanos in October 1984, correspond strikingly with Theophrastus' account of the ancient mines, especially in that they occur in low irregular beds. There are two clay workings shown on the IGME geological map of Samos (Theodoropoulos 1979), one about 700 m due south of Platanos and a second about 1200 m SW of Platanos.

Bentonite (Figs. 37a and b) occurs in an area of volcanic rocks in the west of Samos near Platanos (Fig. 34) and there are existing IGME reports on bentonite deposits in this area. The area of pyroclastic rocks runs N-S and is the only area of the island where such rocks occur. Platanos is a long established vine-growing area and the landscape has been much modified by agriculture (Fig. 35). The area is underlain by volcanics which outcrop in road cuttings south of Platanos where they can be seen to be thinly bedded light-coloured pyroclastic sequences which appear have to been tectonised. In the vicinity of Platanos there is much dense overgrowth which grows rapidly and conceals old walled terraces. However, in some places where new terraces are being created, altered white to greenish bentonitic volcanics have been exposed from under their cover of soil. The rock is distinctly slippery when wet and is known locally as a soap stone. (*sapounochoma*). There was no clear evidence of ancient workings, but the installation of old wash houses are still to be seen in the outskirts of Platanos (see Fig. 36).

Fig. 35 *View of vineyards overlying bentonite deposits in Platanos.*

Fig. 36 *View of Ottoman wash houses in Platanos.*

Fig. 37a (left) *Sample of bentonite similar to that from Platanos, Samos.*
Fig. 37b (right) *SEM image of Samos bentonite from Platanos.*

61

Boron

Boron the element, forms many compounds with diverse modern uses, but it is the borates that are of potential significance in antiquity, i.e. borax and other naturally occurring associated minerals. The main borate minerals are: kernite $Na_2B_4O_6(OH)_3.3H_2O$; borax $Na_2B_4O_5(OH)_4.8H_2O$; ulexite $NaCaB_5O_6(OH)_6.5H_2O$; colemanite $CaB_3O_4(OH)_3.H_2O$; and boracite $Mg_3B_7O_{13}Cl$. The origin of borates does not seem to be well understood. Colemanite (Fig. 38a) is one of the boron industrial minerals which nowadays provide a source of the chemical boron. The borates occur in evaporitic lakes associated with volcanism. The major world deposits are few and are found in the western USA and Turkey. There are small deposits in Greece on Samos (Stamatakis *et al.* 2009) and since borax (or boric acid) has an established use as an eye antiseptic, borates must have been part of one of the Samian Earths (*collyrion*) which was known to be used as an eye salve in antiquity. Localities with potential for borates (a potential antiseptic material in antiquity) and fuller's earth or bentonite (a potential cleansing absorbent clay in antiquity) were sampled, mainly from near Platanos. Water samples taken from a well in the village of Sourides to the NW of Platanos proved undiagnostic. Samples of clear white crystals were collected from Platanos and confirmed by XRD and SEM-EDAX analyses (Fig. 38b) to be the borate mineral colemanite.

Boron minerals could well have been exploited in antiquity. They may have been used for medicinal purposes and being soluble could have been used as an eye salve. One of the early uses of borax, or tincal (natural sodium borate crystals) was as a flux in melting and alloying of metals. It was also used during Babylonian, Egyptian and Mesopotamian times in the process of mummification. The borates are rather like alum; there are many 'fringe' medical websites that promote their use because of established properties, but with little scientific research to support evidence of their antiseptic properties. Garrett (1998) gives an authoritative account of the borates.

Scanning electron microscopy was undertaken to look for any sub-microscopic features or impurities that might be of significance. In some fragments of white crystals only Ca was detected corresponding to calcite or colemanite (Fig. 38a,b) while some crystals contained Ca and S and were therefore very probably gypsum, $CaSO_4.2H_2O$. The presence of gypsum is consistent with the borates occurring in an evaporitic setting. Some of the large white colemanite crystals contained minute inclusions of a phase with Sr and S which is almost certainly celestite, $SrSO_4$, again indicative of a marine evaporitic setting. Chemical analysis with x-ray fluorescence (XRF) analysis of two bulk rock samples was also undertaken to obtain the major

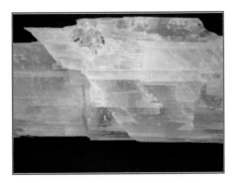 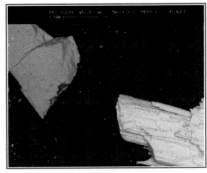

Fig. 38a (left) *Hand specimen of colemanite.* **Fig. 38b (right)** *Scanning electron microscope image (backscattered electron image). The fragment of grey crystal on left is the calcium borate mineral (colemanite), while the bright crystal on the right is gypsum. Scale bar = 1 mm.*

and trace element composition. The bulk rocks were confirmed to be rich in calcium and magnesium and had a large volatile content (loss on ignition) which is consistent with the presence of calcite $CaCO_3$, dolomite $CaMg(CO_3)_2$ and colemanite $Ca_2B_6O_{11}.5(H_2O)$. There was very little soluble material present in the samples, hence little potential for providing special antiseptic properties, especially since the recovered precipitates proved to be calcite. Some of the samples with borates were tested for antiseptic properties but the results proved negative (see box below).

Antiseptic properties

The borate samples were tested for antiseptic properties by Professor Duncan E. Stewart-Tull, Institute of Biomedical and Life Sciences, University of Glasgow. Each sample was used either as the dry powder or as a 1.0 mg suspension in sterile distilled water. Basins (5.0 mm in diameter) were cut in nutrient agar plates supplied with each respective microorganism and filled with either the dry powder or the suspension of the clay. The plates were incubated at 37°C for 24 hours and any zones of inhibition were noted. With microorganisms tested there were no zones of inhibition visible and in some instances growth was actually accentuated around the basin. The organisms used were Pseudomonas aeruginosa, Streptococcus pyogenes and Escherichia coli. It appeared that all the samples tested had no apparent antibacterial activity. Borate-related samples tested included (a) borate whole rock; (b) whole crystals removed from borate rock; (c) ground composite of white crystals from borate rock; (d) re-precipitated soluble salts from water extraction from borate rock (e) boric acid - control. That all the results, including the boric acid control, were negative was especially surprising since boric acid is a well-known antiseptic. Subsequently no further tests were carried out.

Eretrian Earth

Eretria is situated on Euboea, Greece's second largest island after Crete (Figs. 1a and 39). Homer (*Iliad* 2.537) listed Eretria as one of the Greek cities which sent ships to the Trojan War. Based on the name of the Earth, it seems likely that Eretrian Earth came from the vicinity of the Classical city of Eretria, the remains of which occur under the modern town of the same name. We know very little about Eretrian Earth, but it appears to have been well known from antiquity to the middle ages.

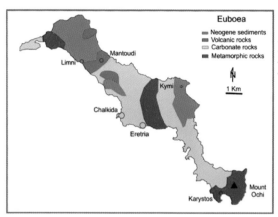

Fig. 39 *Simplified geological map of Euboea showing places mentioned in text.*

We can be confident that it was a white earth that was used in medicinal preparations. It is mentioned in Pliny and Dioscorides but not in Theophrastus nor Strabo; its absence in Strabo's writing is strange because he wrote extensively on Euboea and its natural resources particularly in reference to its asbestos quarries in Karystos. Higgins and Higgins (1996, 87) refer to asbestos, recovered from veins in serpentinite on Mt Ochi in SE Euboea, being used in antiquity for making fire-proof cloth.

Eretrian Earth (*terra eretria*) is also known as *creta eretria*. Pliny (*Nat. Hist.* XXXIII.163) uses *terra Eretria* and *Eretria creta* interchangeably, but Stephanides (1898) suggests that *creta* is a fine earth thus encompassing other substances apart from aluminosilicates (clays). Bailey (1929; and commentary by Levidis 1994, 225) proposes that Eretrian Earth was magnesite, $MgCO_3$, given the proximity of the deposits to the town.

It was white and still known and classified as a white substance in the mid-18th century by Da Costa (1757): "*It is a fine and pure earth, of a greyish white, moderately heavy, and of a smooth surface, not colouring the hands, and readily crumbling between the fingers, it adheres firmly to the tongue, and melts easily in the mouth, leaving a lasting smoothness on it, without the least harshness between the teeth."* Da Costa provides a clue to its source: *"It is dug in the Negropont, near the ancient Eretria, and might be had in quantities if it were brought into use in medicine, as it anciently was, and its peculiar alkaline quality might very well recommend it to be at present".* And Da Costa adds: *"The ancients were extremely careful in their manner of preparing it for use; a description of the method is given at length by Dioscorides, and amounts to a very fine way of levigating, analogous to that by which we now prepare testaceous (shelly) powders. It stands recommended as a noble astringent and sudorific* (produces sweat)".

Euboea has endured a complex tectonic history and consists mainly of metamorphic schists, serpentinites and marbles (Higgins and Higgins 1996). There are three areas in the north and centre of the island with basin-shaped deposits of Neogene calcareous lacustrine sediments; these low-lying areas have developed fertile soils. Lignite and bauxite deposits occur on the island, and marble was exploited in central/southern Euboea in Roman times. The island has been a major producer of magnesite. For properties of Eretrian clay see Jones (1986, 144) (Figs. 40, 41).

Fig. 40 *View of the giant clay mine at Vasiliko in the Lelantine Plain between Chalkis and Eretria, 10 km west of Eretria used by brick and tile makers (picture taken in mid 1980s).*

Fig. 41 *The picture shows the way farmers in this area used to sell their 'topsoil' to brick makers. The clay deposit has been removed to the level of c. 3 m, as can be gauged from the scale inserted here for comparison between the*  *small house in the background and the depth of the deposit. In the foreground there are vineyards which testify to the fertility of the soil lost for ever to the brickeries.*

Cleigenis' Soap

In the 1960s, in the hastily and anarchically expanding modern city of Athens, amidst optimism and confidence for the future, after a world war *and* a civil war, there was one local detergent company which was doing particularly well out of the boom. The company was called Vianyl and the product they were promoting was called ROL (ToVima 2010). As part of their advertising campaign, the company commissioned the editor of a well-established children's magazine, Georgia Tarsouli, to write a series of children's books titled *I was also there,* which they distributed free with the purchase of their product. The protagonist was a young boy called Alkis who would travel back in time and find himself the accidental bystander in some crucial event in the history of ancient Egypt or Babylon, Byzantium or Crete. The books were very well written; they left a lot to the imagination while at the same time informing their young audiences. A hefty dose of poetic license was applied, since Alkis would be transported back, in a time machine, as a result of his archaeologist uncle's experiments with radiocarbon dating (!). But the most memorable part was perhaps the description of how Alkis would 'land' back in his bed, in the present and invariably be woken up by the loud sound of the cement mixer operating in the plot next door. This was a period when a multitude of small developers would raise, in record time, blocks of flats in tiny plots within the city's narrow streets. The description of Alkis' sudden 'flight' back is probably one of the few instances where the sounds of the city's 'recent antiquity' have been so vividly preserved for posterity. Perhaps against all expectations, fifty years on, these children's books (a series of about ten) are now considered both pioneering and classic in their approach and outlook.

Washing powders are perhaps, together with perfumes, amongst the most 'intimate' of archaeological artefacts, more than pottery, metal or glass. As contributors to the personal hygiene of all members of the social scale, in the home or the public baths, together with medicines, they sustained good health and well being. Detergents are defined as cleaning substances made from synthetic chemical compounds rather than fats and lye, which were the main ingredients of the washing powders of antiquity. Lye is the liquid produced from the leaching (slow percolation of water) through wood ashes. But although fat and lye constitute the main ingredients of soap, we know that other mineral-based substances like Kimolian Earth were used in the public baths (*valaneia*) in Athens in the 4th century BC, as well as by fullers in the fulleries for the degreasing of woollen cloth. The lye provided the alkalis, sodium and potassium, the fat the fatty acids, and the Kimolian Earth,

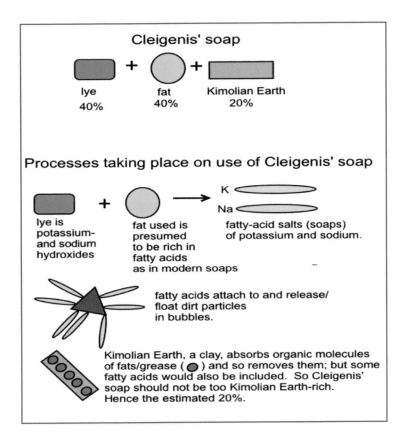

Cleigenis' soap

lye 40%   fat 40%   Kimolian Earth 20%

Processes taking place on use of Cleigenis' soap

lye is potassium- and sodium hydroxides

fat used is presumed to be rich in fatty acids as in modern soaps

K — Na — fatty-acid salts (soaps) of potassium and sodium.

fatty acids attach to and release/ float dirt particles in bubbles.

Kimolian Earth, a clay, absorbs organic molecules of fats/grease (●) and so removes them; but some fatty acids would also be included. So Cleigenis' soap should not be too Kimolian Earth-rich. Hence the estimated 20%.

Fig. 42 *Schematic illustration of the composition of Cleigenis' soap and how it might have worked. The component parts are estimated.*

the absorbing clay. The processes taking place in using Cleigenis soap are shown in Fig. 42. Aristophanes in his *Frogs* pokes fun at one such *valanefs*, the owner of an Athenian baths establishment, but also a local politician, Cleigenis; Cleigenis is a baboon, Aristophanes says, and it is not clear whether he refers to the man's looks or his personality or both. Fullers suffered from exposure to both sulphur used in bleaching as well as caustic soda and the ingredients shown in the soaps of antiquity like that used for Cleigenis (see Fig. 42). The purpose of Kimolian Earth is to absorb organic molecules of fat or grease. But, because fatty acids formed by the reaction of lye and fat have similar composition, Kimolian Earth would also remove them, and so the concentration of Kimolian Earth would need to be measured. Too much lye would make the washing powder caustic and too much fat would make it 'slimy'; finally too much earth would render it 'muddy'.

Kimolian Earth

Kimolos (or Cimolos) (Fig. 43), a small island close to north-eastern Melos in the SW Cyclades, is, like Melos, dominated by volcanic rocks. But, also like Melos, there is no record of recent nor modern volcanic activity, although hot springs occur on the NE of the island (at Prassa). The remains of the ancient capital of Kimolos, Hellinika (or Ellinika), are to be found submerged in the west of the island. Kimolian Earth was first mentioned by Theophrastus (*On Stones* 62) but only briefly; he does not describe its properties or uses and only hints at the fact that it was used for degreasing cloth. Yet his father is reputed to have been a fuller and so as a child he would have had a personal knowledge of the material itself (Robertson 1986). Kimolos has also been called Argentiera, and confusingly there is an earth named *Creta argentaria,* the difference between the two earths being negligible. *Creta argentaria* was possibly a commercial name given to Kimolian Earth used for polishing silver; unlike Melos, there is no silver mineralisation on the island which may have justified the name. Pliny (*Nat. Hist.* XXXV.199) mentions that *creta argentaria* was used in the hippodrome to mark the finishing line but also to paint the feet of the slaves they brought to the market for sale. It was, he says, of the lowest quality.

Clay that had been used for cleaning cloth for thousands of years came to be known as fuller's earth throughout Europe and is now known as the absorbing clay bentonite which consists mainly of the clay mineral montmorillonite (Robertson 1986, 1-5). The clay works by absorbing oil and grease and removing it from the cloth. Fuller's earth was used especially for degreasing wool and preparing it for spinning and dyeing, but its absorbing properties led to additional uses such as in cosmetics and household cleaners (Robertson 1986, 147-170). Bentonite continues to be in much demand as an industrial mineral for uses as diverse as drilling-muds and cat litter. We associate fuller's earth/bentonite with Kimolian Earth rather than Lemnian Earth but Galen's observation cannot be ignored. It presumes that these materials occurred in association with one another at least in some localities.

Apart from degreasing sheep's wool, fuller's earth was also used as a medicine (Strabo X.5.1). Dioscorides (V.176) states that it was white or purple hued and was used for treating tumours and inflammation. However, it was also used for bites, swellings, tumours, as an ingredient in an eye salve (Columella VI.17.4; Theophrastus *On Stones*.62; Dioscorides V.156; Pliny *Nat. Hist.* XXXV.195-8; *Nat. Hist.* XXXVIII.110), and also a styptic (Celsus V.1).

While travelling in the Cyclades in 1750, Maihows equated Kimolian Earth with fuller's earth found in Bedfordshire (Maihows 1763, 276). When John Galt was on Hydra in 1810 he reported that he *"met here with the Cimolian Earth. It is however common enough, and is brought from Milo in boat loads, for sale. I am no judge of such things, but I think it only a better sort of fuller's earth. The common people use it as a substitute for soap, and it does very well. It costs little more than a penny a pound"* (Galt 1813, 245).

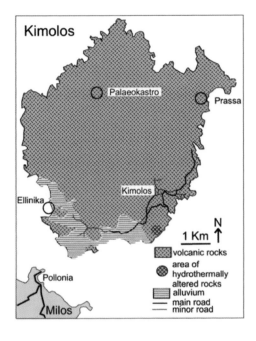

Fig. 43 *Geological map of Kimolos showing places mentioned in the text.*

Robertson (1986) provides a detailed account of fuller's earth from antiquity to modern times. Beneke and Lagaly (2002) differentiate between bleaching earths and Kimolian Earth. Bleaching earth or clay is clay used for removing impurities, usually from oil. However, Kimolian Earth (bentonite) would be expected to act in the same way since it would remove grease/fat/oil from skin when used as a soap and from wool when used by fullers. So if the clay is rich in bentonite, there should be no need for any additional components but zeolites (see glossary) would help the process. In antiquity soap was traditionally made from the lixiviation of ashes mixed with animal fat as a binder (Simmons and Appleton 2007).

Fuller's earth is a European term but the American term bentonite is in more common use for the same type of material and is the modern name used commercially worldwide (e.g. O'Driscoll 1989; Kendall 1996). Bentonite is a type of clay-rich sediment or sedimentary rock that is known to be rich in the mineral montmorillonite, and Melos happens to be one of the world's major sources. It is clearly commercial dominance that has led to the adoption worldwide of the name bentonite, named after Fort Benton in the United States where it was discovered and produced on a large scale. The name bentonite has also been adopted geologically for this type of rock. Given its name it is almost certain that outcrops of bentonite, albeit

69

now greatly modified by quarrying on the south coast of Kimolos and readily visible on arrival by ferry-boat, provided this early source of special clay -rich sediment with useful properties. It seems inevitable that it was also available in surface outcrops on Melos and probably other islands in the Aegean. Kimolos is very close to Melos and hence similar in its geological history. Kimolos is an island dominated by young (Pliocene) volcanic rocks (Fig. 43) which range in age from about 1 to 3.5 Ma (Fytikas and Vougiou-kalakis 1993; Christidis 1998). Felsic lava flows and pyroclastic rocks cover much of the island and result in its rugged hilly topography.

As on Melos, the volcanic rocks have been extensively hydrothermally altered, and this has led to the formation of bentonite which has been extensively exploited until relatively recently. Hydrothermal processes have also led to the formation of zeolitic tuffs (containing mordenite and some clinoptilite) which are more abundant in the SW of the island (Fragoulis *et al.* 1997). Such zeolitic rocks have potential uses as absorbents and as pozzolanic additives in cements (Fragoulis *et al.* 1997) but are unlikely to have had any significance in antiquity. While bentonite is usually greenish grey, white bentonite (Christidis and Scott 1997) is found on Kimolos and this could well be significant in relation to the nature of Kimolian Earth. In the south and south-west (Fig. 43) and in the extreme NE of the island, there are some extensive low-lying areas occupied mainly by alluvial deposits making these potential areas for early occupation and farming.

Chian Earth

We know little of Chian Earth other than it was a white earth similar to that of Samian Earth and had cosmetic/skin-care uses (Pliny *Nat. Hist.* XXXV.56). It is also mentioned briefly by Dioscorides (Book V.174) who also adds that it is comparable to Samian Earth and "*it makes the face and whole body wrinkle free and clear*". It seems probable that because of its colour, uses on skin and similarity to Samian Earth, that it was montmorillonite rich material. Hasluck (1909-10, 220) quoting earlier sources reports that Chian Earth was as beneficial as Lemnian Earth and was to be found near Pyrgi in the centre of the island. Chios (Figs. 1a and 1b) is a large island in the north-eastern Aegean close to the Turkish Mainland with a rich history in the post-Byzantine period. The main archaeological site on Chios is Emporio in the south of the island, a complex multi-phase settlement dating from the Neolithic to the Archaic period (Boardman 1967). That Chian transport amphorae have been found throughout the Mediterranean (Whitbread 1995) attests to the island's wine industry, but in recent times

Chios is known as an exporter of mastic. There are indications of ancient volcanic rocks on the island (Beccaluva *et al.* 2007) which could potentially be altered to bentonite, and there is indeed bentonite in Chios (Christidis 1992; Christidis *et al.* 1997) (Fig. 44). Chian Earth, if it consists of bentonite, would be derived from such deposits. To our knowledge, no work has been undertaken to search for Chian Earth on the island.

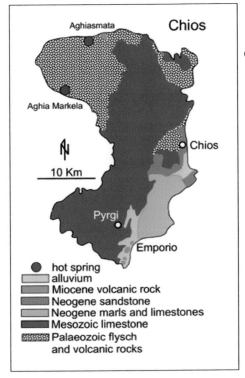

Fig 44. *The geological map of Chios.*

Apelles' Palette

Apelles was perhaps antiquity's most celebrated artist, a painter who lived in the 4th century BC. Pliny had the highest regard for him.

"But it was Apelles of Cos, in the hundred and twelfth Olympiad" (c. 330 BC)*"who surpassed all the other painters who either preceded or succeeded him. Single-handed, he contributed more to painting than all the others together, and even went so far as to publish some treatises on the*

principles of the art" (Pliny *Nat. Hist.* XXXV.36; trans. Bostock and Riley 1855).

His paintings were so vivid and life-like that Pliny narrates a story told in *"the writings of Apion, the grammarian, (.... who) seems altogether incredible. One of those persons,"* he says, *"who divine events by the traits of the features, and are known as 'metoposcopi'* (physiognomists) *was enabled, by an examination of his* (Apelles) *portraits, to tell the year of their death, whether past or future,* (and) *of each person represented"* (Pliny *Nat. Hist.* XXXV.79). It was Apelles, Pliny suggests, who together with other famous artists introduced and maintained the practice of *tetrachromia* or the use of four essential colours in the artist's palette: red, white, yellow and black. He praises these artists of the past and laments the demise of the art of painting presumably due to the use of cheap materials brought from far away lands. The reason, he concludes, is that people nowadays go for the material value of things rather than their spiritual value:

"With only four colours– from the whites, the Melian Earth, from the yellows, the attic ochres (sil), from the reds, the sinopic (miltos) from the Pontus, and from the blacks, atramentum, did Apelles, Aetion, Melanthios and Nicomachos, these most glorious of painters execute their immortal works. Now that they are applying purple to walls and India is providing us with the silt of its rivers, the blood of its snakes and its elephants, nowadays the art of painting has lost its value" (Pliny *Nat. Hist.* XXXV.53; trans from Levidis (1994, 58) by EPJ).

Pliny's *Tetrachromia* did not include the colour blue, presumably on the grounds that it could be produced from black; furthermore there were other earlier *tetrachromias* reported, with different combinations of colours like that by Demokritos in the 5th century BC which included white, black, red and green (Gage 1999, 29; Gombrich 1976). Sinopic *miltos* was already famous in antiquity from the time of Theophrastus (*On Stones* 62) who considered Keian to be the best, but by Pliny's time their relative importance or commercial availability seem to have been reversed. In this book we will concentrate on the red *miltos* of Kea and the white Earth of Melos, two of the four pigments in Apelles' palette.

The colour red: *Miltos* of Kea

Kea is a small island in the Northern Cyclades which enjoyed considerable economic and cultural prosperity intermittently from the Bronze Age to the Hellenistic period (Mendoni and Mazarakis-Ainian 1998). The Bronze Age site of Aghia Irini, excavated by Caskey (1971; 1972) in the late 1960s spans the Minoan and Mycenaean periods. Despite its small size, Kea during the 6th century BC was home to four separate city states, namely Korissia, Ioulis, Karthaia and Poiessa. The excavations at Karthaia revealed an acropolis, public buildings, temples, a theatre and fortifications (Simandoni-Bournia *et al.* 2009). Three of the city states, Korissia, Ioulis and Karthaia, minted their own silver coinage, in addition to the *Koinon* of the Keans (a coinage representing all city states). They continued to mint until the 1st century BC (Papageorgiadou-Banis 1997). Kea had good agricultural soil, but its richness in mineral deposits, including *miltos*, was a likely additional factor of its prosperity.

Miltos was a valuable commodity and a material used primarily as a pigment, and this included shipbuilding to paint ships red. We can infer that it was available in bulk and must have been worked on a relatively large scale. However, because iron oxides were readily available on mainland Greece, for example in the neighbouring lead-mining area of Laurion, Keian *miltos* must have had some special property that made it especially desirable. This importance is confirmed by the existence of a special treaty between the city states of Kea and Athens dating to the 4th century BC which decreed that *miltos* had to be exported only to Athens, on Athenian ships and without any duty levied on it. The export of *miltos* to other destinations was prohibited under penalty of death. The fact that nearly all city states could export *miltos* to Athens must imply that each had access to its own supplies (Mendoni and Mazarakis-Ainian 1998).

Theophrastus (*On Stones* 52-3) stated that Keian *miltos* was the best and it came from iron mines. He added (*On Stones* 53) that *miltos* could be produced artificially but it was of inferior quality and reported the incident with a certain Cydias, who was credited with the development of the synthetic *miltos* when he noticed that when a general store was destroyed by fire, half burnt ochre had turned red. There were three kinds of *miltos*, namely deep red, pale and intermediate. Most classical authors agree that there was at least one other major locality for *miltos*, namely Sinope, on the north coast of Turkey, although this could be where it was processed/exported rather than mined. Here we reinforce our case that it was a red iron oxide and contained fine-grained hematite, ferric oxide Fe_2O_3 (Photos-Jones *et al.* 1997). However, the exceptional value and uses of *miltos* indicated that it was something other than typical common hematite.

Pigment aside, *miltos* is also purported to have medicinal properties. Aetius Amidenus, who lived *c.* AD 530-60 in Alexandria and Constantinople, wrote an extant medical encyclopaedia called the *Tetrabiblon*, so called for its division into four sections. According to Aetius (*Libri medicinales* II.5) *miltos* was astringent (*styptike*) and a drying agent (*anaxerantike*), and could also be applied as a poultice (*emplastike*) around the eyes to stop watering, or taken in a drink to stop the spitting of blood (Olivieri 1935). This continuum of applications from pigment to eye salve, although seemingly far fetched, echoes current research into fine iron oxides.

Our search for Keian *miltos* naturally began with a search for iron deposits and old mines. There are many old underground workings on Kea including Orkos, the cave of Trypospilies, Spathi and Spasmata (Fig. 45). However, it is not easy to date such workings as later exploitation tends to destroy evidence of earlier workings. Nevertheless, archaeological survey (Mendoni and Mazarakis-Ainian 1998) of Trypospilies cave revealed evidence of working in the Classical period in the form of 4th century BC pottery sherds. Although there was modern working of iron ore at Orkos, early in the 20th century, it is still the best place to see potential *miltos* in the field (Figs. 45 and 46).

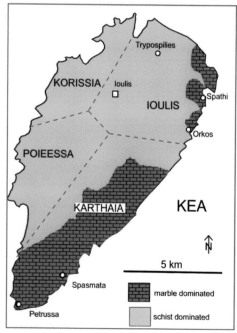

Fig. 45 *Simplified geological map of Kea showing the approximate boundaries between ancient city states (Cherry et al. 1991) and areas with the main rock types, (after Cottier 1996). Sites with mineralisation that feature in this account are also shown. The small modern capital of the island (Ioulis) is indicated and the main port lies in the large bay to the NW of the town. There are few roads on the island. The coastline generally consists of steep cliffs with many small bays.*

The Orkos iron ore deposit is located on the east side of Kea in a small outlier of the main marble-rich area identified on the geological map of Kea (IGME 1982) (Fig. 45). The style of iron mineralisation is similar to the deposit at Spasmata but it is larger with more extensive workings (Figs. 46 and 47). At both localities there are natural cavern developments above the mine galleries. Such caverns are common in calcareous rocks (e.g. limestone caves) and if they were developed into mines in antiquity this would result in an old mineral working which is difficult to interpret. Cottier (1996) who explored the mines found iron oxyhydroxides and calcite at Orkos. Neither siderite nor iron-sulphide minerals, the expected precursors to secondary iron minerals, were found. A polished thin section of iron oxide is shown (Fig.48b).

There is little variation in rock type on Kea. The island is composed mainly of metamorphic rocks, schists and marbles in a general SW-NE trend (IGME 1982). The schists formed as a result of regional metamorphism during deep burial of sediments and volcanics at the end of the Mesozoic. This metamorphism produced high pressure 'blueschist' metamorphic facies rocks throughout the Aegean. However, the rocks were later heated at lower pressure producing lower pressure 'green' chloritic schist (Blake *et al.* 1981; Dixon and Robertson 1984).

Fig. 46 *Orkos. View of entrance to coastal quarry, looking N.*

Fig. 47 *Plan of Orkos quarry (after Cottier 1996) showing the coastal setting. The workings to the north-east were not explored. The schistose rocks are thrust over the marble so the marble lies at depth under the road.*

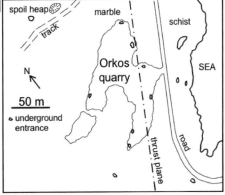

Although simply called 'schist', the Keian metamorphic rocks vary in grain size and texture from coarse gneissose rocks to finer phyllites. They contain muscovite, calcite and chlorite as the dominant minerals. Rocks that were originally volcanic in origin are dark green and richer in chlorite. The marbles are bluish grey and represent metamorphosed limestones that were interbedded with the sediments that provided the schistose rocks. There are also some younger limestones which occur mainly in the extreme north of the island for example at Trypospilies. Iron enrichments occur near the contact of schist and marble and this is true for all the underground workings The iron enrichments appear to have formed in two stages. A primary stage when hydrothermal fluids, which are rising through fractures in rocks towards the Earth's surface, precipitate minerals through cooling and/or reaction with reactive rocks such as marble and cool fluids in fractures in the rock. The best evidence of this stage is in the south of Kea where fluorite, galena and baryte mineralisation is found, but there is no pyrite nor siderite which would have been expected as primary minerals with the potential to produce secondary iron minerals. It is the iron mineralization rather than iron-lead that is of interest here, and a short discussion on iron oxide-oxyhydroxide minerals follows.

Hematite, Fe_2O_3, is a very common iron oxide mineral that is distinctly red when very fine-grained (micron size). However, coarse-grained hematite is metallic grey and an important ore mineral of iron; this type of hematite would have to be ground to produce a pigment. Fine natural red hematite is common worldwide; occurring, for example, in lateritic soils. It can also form on hydrothermal alteration of rocks. Hematite is anhydrous - i.e. free of water. On the other hand, the more common amorphous to semi-crystalline iron oxyhydroxides are yellowish brown in colour and contain both structural and molecular water (e.g. limonite, $FeOOH \cdot nH_2O$). It is well known that such yellowish-brown iron oxyhydroxides turn red on heating because they lose water and are converted to ferric oxide (hematite); this relationship has been particularly important in our study of *miltos* (see Photos-Jones *et al*. 1997). The transition of limonite powder (yellow brown) to hematite (red) on heating can be represented by the equation:

$$2FeOOH \cdot nH_2O \longrightarrow Fe_2O_3 + (n+1)H_2O$$

In the north of Kea the iron deposits are dominated by iron oxyhydroxides such as goethite which are typical of secondary enrichment processes and may have formed by replacement of pyrite and/or siderite. However, they could well be 'primary' rather than resulting from a 'secondary' process (Photos-Jones *et al*. 1997); for example, if the uprising hydrothermal solutions mixed with oxidising surface waters, any reduced ferrous iron (Fe^{2+})

in the hydrothermal solution would be precipitated as it was oxidised to ferric iron (Fe^{3+}). The significance of understanding such possible processes is that it can help us appreciate the nature of the deposits worked in antiquity and which have now disappeared. Such iron precipitates would be expected to range in colour from yellow-brown (ochres - limonite/goethite) to reddish (fine-grained hematite). While all these minerals contain only ferric iron, the ochres in contrast to hematite contain structural and molecular water. This is reflected in their formulae:

limonite = $FeOOH.nH_2O$; goethite = $FeOOH$; hematite = Fe_2O_3

In fact, the variety of colours typical of these iron oxides is clearly visible at Orkos (Photos-Jones *et al.* 1997; Fig. 48a). Powder XRD analysis is a relatively simple analytical method to use to characterise such minerals (Photos-Jones *et al.* 1997, 365, Fig. 2), although it is not easy to detect small amounts of hematite within ochres, for example by using XRD. Chemical analyses demonstrated the presence of manganese in the Trypospilies sample which probably corresponds to its purplish colour. Examination using scanning electron microscopy confirmed that the Orkos red material is indeed very fine-grained (Photos-Jones *et al.* 1997). The 'red ochres' are quite soft and amenable to grinding.

  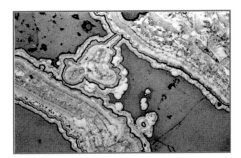

Fig. 48a *(left) Keian red miltos and yellow ochre from Orkos.*
Fig. 48b *(right) polished section of Orkos goethite.*

Artefactual evidence for ore grinding within the mine was found at Trypospilies (L Mendoni *pers. comm.*). It may be that it was the presence of calcite in the iron oxyhydroxides that made them particularly suitable for use as pigments. Although some preliminary experiments demonstrated its potential quality as a pigment for paint, for example the excellent staining power of 'Orkos red', the potential benefit of calcite in *miltos* paint used for buildings - probably in wall paintings and shipbuilding - is worthy of further investigation.

The colour white: The white rock of Melos

Melos in the SW Cyclades is one of the most extensively mined islands in the Aegean and a leading exporter of bentonite and other industrial minerals (Stamatakis *et al.* 1996). Most authors agree that Melian Earth was white and used as a white pigment. Theophrastus (*On Stones* 62) thought it was white, rough, not greasy and had a loose texture. Dioscorides (*De Materia Medica* V.180), on the other hand, stated that it was ash-coloured like Eretrian Earth, rough and was good for 'extending' painters' colours as well as green plasters. Compared to Samian Earth, Melian Earth felt rough (probably the result of the presence of silica, the mineral cristobalite) and when it was rubbed between the fingers it made a sound just like pumice (Stephanides 1898). Presumably if the silica content was high it could have had good abrasive powers and be used as a polishing powder as well.

Any visitor to Melos travelling inland or around the island by boat is soon aware that white to cream-coloured rock (see Fig. 49) is widespread in the landscape. Among the many types of light-coloured rock, it is the white rock altered by geothermal activity that is significant here and which we have called 'altered white rock'. Melos is commonly called a volcanic island as the rocks are mainly young volcanic rocks; lava-producing volcanic activity is thought to have been long extinct but geothermal phenomena such as phreatic explosions, hot springs and solfataras continued long after the initial human occupation of the island (Fytikas 1989).

Fig. 49 *White rock (volcanic tuff) of Melos at Sarakiniko bay.*

The soft *altered* white rocks of Melos were formed through hydrothermal alteration. Analyses of these white rocks have shown that they contain kaolin and alunite and free silica in the form of the minerals quartz and/or cristobalite and sometimes native sulphur. The rocks are altered in the sense that they were usually not originally white and consisted of different minerals. Alteration has come about on account of a network of fractures which are filled with hot water vapour in the sort of setting that would be expected underneath a modern geyser field (Fig. 50).

These hot acidic fluids are related to the long-extinct volcanism on Melos. They exist at depth but can come to the surface as hot springs. Together with localised minor emissions of hot sulphurous vapours, they provide the surface expression of the volcano-related geothermal processes so common in many parts of the Aegean. The vapour has leached soluble metals out of the rock to produce kaolin and leave residual silica which has a low solubility. This is a well-known process called 'acid-sulphate alteration' which takes its name from acidic sulphate-rich solutions that occur at depth in volcanic areas.

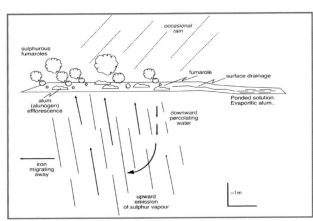

Fig. 50 *Hot fluids circulating under solfatara (simplified after Hall et al. 2003a).*

The outline of the geology of Melos, taken from Hall *et al.* (2003b), provides a brief overview with explanatory notes of the geological setting and major rock types on Melos (Fig. 51) and a means to understand the mechanism of formation of Melian Earth. Melos forms part of a calc-alkaline volcanic arc which is an arc-shaped distribution of relatively young or active volcanoes across the Aegean that have lavas and associated volcanic products with a range in chemical composition that indicates a relatively shallow origin of melting and magma development in the Earth's crust and tends to be associated with explosive volcanism. The volcanism is related to subduction, the dipping down and progressive but slow movement of a few centimetres per year, of the African plate, the large part of the Earth's crust that contains the African continent, northwards under the plate

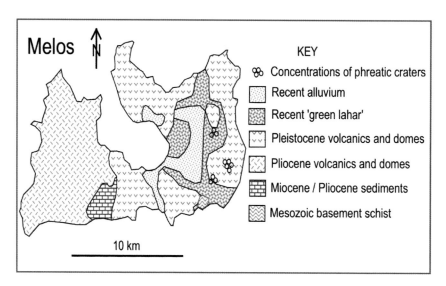

Fig. 51 *Simplified geology of Melos after Fytikas (1977).*

that contains the Aegean area (Robertson and Dixon 1984; Fytikas *et al.* 1984). This means that Melos is in a geologically active area, in a zone of recent and active volcansim that extends through the Aegean. The Aegean is also an area of frequent earthquakes due to earth movements related to the deformation of the colliding plates. The metamorphic basement (the assemblage of relatively young rocks that underlies the entire Aegean area) is only partially exposed and the surface geology of the island is dominated by Tertiary and Quaternary hydrothermally altered felsic volcanic rocks (Fytikas 1977; Shelford 1982; Plimer and Petrou 2000) (Fig. 51). The metamorphic rocks, formed at great depth in the Earth's crust at high temperatures and pressures, were then uplifted to the surface as a result of the colliding plates. The volcanic rocks on Melos are quite young (a hundred thousand to a few million years old) and relict volcanic features such as lava flows and craters formed of volcanic ash/tuff are still visible in places.

There is some present-day minor geothermal activity resulting from hot-rock at depth, both on-shore (mainly fumaroles) and off-shore (escaping hot gases) with the high geothermal gradient focused on Zephyria (Fytikas 1989; Botz *et al.* 1996) (Fig. 52). So Melos is a 'hot-spot' on the Earth's crust with sub-surface temperatures high enough to boil water at depths of tens of metres or less in places. The island's potential for geothermal energy has been assessed and a pilot plant developed but subsequently abandoned; although now a ruin, it is part of the interesting 'industrial heritage' of the search for geothermal energy that is found throughout south/central Melos. The lack of surface water on the island limits the present-day expression of

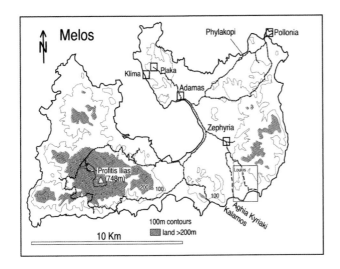

Fig. 52 *Melos showing places mentioned in text.*

geothermally-related phenomena such as hot springs. However, although there is ample evidence of hot-water having been found at the surface on Melos in the past (e.g. former hot 'baths') and it is certainly present at depth, if there is little rainfall then there is no source of water for inland hot springs. One of the geological challenges when such geothermal activity is present in an area is to establish whether or not the area is still at the post-volcanic stage of cooling down or at an early stage of heating up due to magma at depth that might eventually erupt in a new volcanic episode.

The white earth of Melos: Melian Earth

Melian Earth is also mentioned by Vitruvius (VII.7.3), Plutarch (*De Def. Or.* 436c), and Pliny (*Nat. Hist.* XXXV.188). In *De Natura Fossilium* Agricola rather dismisses it as a mere white to intermediate earth used by painters (Bandy and Bandy 1955, 30). It is most likely that Melian Earth was white and that the grey variety, when available, may have been used as a medicine (Bailey 1929; Levidis 1994). It is also possible that, although Melian Earth was for long considered to be a good white pigment, by the 16th century it had either been displaced by other white pigments such as lead carbonate and/or there was no longer a source or need for the best quality white Melian Earth (Levidis 1994, 211).

What qualities would be required of a white pigment such as Melian Earth? Pigments are used to give colour to paints, for which qualities such as high

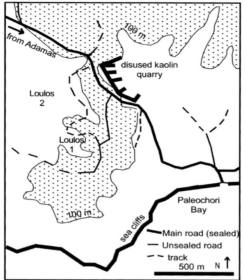

Fig. 53 *Map of Loulos, SE Melos.*

covering power, bright intense colour, ability to mix with other pigments and ability to be applied uniformly are highly desirable. Kaolin, known more commonly as china clay, is a modern white pigment which happens to be one of the minerals that features prominently in white altered rocks on Melos. It therefore seems logical to accept that it was at least a major component in Melian Earth. Analysis showed that the Loulos deposits (Figs. 53 and 54) consisted of kaolin with varying amounts of silica and alunite.

Fig. 54 *Old workings at Loulos, SE Melos*

82

Analysis of kaolin-rich white rock from Melos (McNulty 2000) revealed in addition to the main constituent of kaolin, some silica (in the form of the mineral quartz or cristobalite) as well as some alunite (a rare whitish mineral that contains potassium, aluminium and sulphate). This is an observation consistent with Dioscorides' comment that when rubbed it feels gritty (due to the presence of quartz inclusions). Caley and Richards (1956) suggest that Melian Earth was millowite on account of its silica content. Levidis' experiments with white earths from Melos showed that kaolin was greasy and difficult to use with a paint (Levidis 1994, 211). However, we consider that the key to understanding Melian Earth is that it is a white pigment with good covering power because of its high kaolin content.

Melian Earth was used extensively in antiquity as a white pigment. It is likely that Melian Earth came from the altered white rocks of which there are several possibilities: an entire rock; one mineral or a rock dominated by one mineral; a processed rock with a modified mineralogical composition. In any case, altered white rock occurs in abundance throughout SE Melos. These rocks are rich in kaolin that would provide the white colour and the basic requirements of a white pigment such as softness and covering power. However, the altered white rocks of Melos also contain potentially deleterious components such as relatively coarse quartz, cristobalite, alunite and at times possibly alum minerals and similar soluble mineral salts such as halite (sodium chloride as in sea salt) and Epsom salts (magnesium sulphates). These additional minerals would have led to variable qualities of material used as white pigment from Melos and its eventual replacement in the 'world market' by alternatives.

Earths but not in name: Melian alum and sulphur

Alum has primarily been used as a mordant. A first reference to alum (*stypteria*) appears to be in the Linear B tablets dating to 1400 BC from Knossos (Perna 2005) and for use in textiles. This suggests that the Mycenaeans were trading in alum and must have established the 'technology' for its extraction well before that time. Melian alum and sulphur are two minerals treated at length as part of our forthcoming publication (Photos-Jones and Hall *in press*) so they are presented here in summary form and to complete the discussion on the earths of the Aegean. Singer (1948) reviewed the history of alum and its development as a chemical to meet mainly the needs of the dyeing industry. Pliny considered the *alumen* of Melos to be one of the best, if not the best (*Nat. Hist.* XXXV.184,188). He describes eight different varieties (three liquid and five solid, each with its distinct physical properties and applications). Establishing the modern mineralogy of each of the different species is a complex process and involves laboratory-based tasks requiring chemical and mineralogical investigation as well as reconsideration of interpretations of his description of each type of '*alumen*'. Our work on Melos, a major producer of alum in antiquity, has helped to establish the nature of Melian *alumen* (Hall *et al.* 2003a; Hall and Photos-Jones 2005; Photos-Jones and Hall 2010) and provides much of the content on alum in this book. There are two potential sources of alum on Melos, from alunite and from fumaroles.

Alum from alunite: Alunite is mined for the manufacture of alum. Accepting that the *alumen* of antiquity was rich in an aluminium sulphate mineral led us to look for alunite $(KAl_3(SO_4)_2(OH))$, which occurs as hard, white, fine granular masses in trachytic and allied volcanic rocks. It is a hydrated basic aluminium and potassium sulphate which is soluble in sulphuric acid but not water. Alum is prepared from alunite by prolonged roasting and lixiviation and subsequent crystallization by evaporation. It is relatively difficult to produce alum from alunite and the technology was not in widespread use until post-Roman times. A method involving roasting and repeated slaking is well known to have been used in medieval times (Singer 1948, 229 Fig. 132). A change in ratios of components and removal of $Al^{...}$ presumably as an insoluble aluminium hydroxide is required as shown in the following possible reaction:

$$KAl_3(SO_4)_2(OH)_6 + 12H_2O \longrightarrow KAl(SO_4)_2.12\ H_2O + 2Al(OH)_3$$

alunite   K-alum

No archaeological evidence for alunite processing such as structures, fuel or waste has been found on Melos (Photos-Jones *et al.* 1999), but alunite does exist in association with deep vein sulphur. It is almost certain that this deep alunite was not being mined in antiquity and instead Pliny's *alumen* (alum) was most likely to be efflorescences associated with fumaroles in solfataras (Fig. 55).

Alum from fumaroles: There is an easy means of retrieving - actually harvesting since the source is renewable - alum which is scraping and packaging of natural efflorescences. While many white efflorescences occur on the white rocks of Melos (see section on Melian Earth), for example in rock-cut caverns, it is not easy to identify the particular chemical compound/mineral in the field. They all appear as white efflorescences, but upon analysis they may prove to be magnesium sulphate (Epsom salts) or calcium sulphate (gypsum), for example. However, good samples of white efflorescences that were rich in aluminium sulphate were obtained from active, or recently active, open-air fumarole sites. These are very obvious both on account of the soil discoloration and the mild to strong sulphurous smell. Soluble aluminium sulphate therefore occurs in three ways on Melos (Photos-Jones and Hall *in press*):

a. as low temperature efflorescences in caves/mines in white rock (altered silicate rocks with kaolin, silica and alunite)
b. as efflorescences at sulphurous fumaroles in the open air
c. as efflorescences at sulphurous fumaroles in caves/mines

Fig. 55 *Solfatara at Aghia Kyriaki, SE Melos (Fig. 52), characterised by grey white, sulphurous smelling patch of dry land.*

Small easily worked deposits of alum would have been readily found in Roman times close to active fumaroles in the post-volcanic landscape of SE Melos. Sub-surface deposits could have been exploited as fumaroles were followed underground. Such mines were indeed worked in SE Melos by the 17th century as we know from eye-witness accounts. From our fieldwork, mineralogical and chemical analyses, experimental work and in consideration of its uses, we are confident that this alum was mainly the aluminium sulphate mineral alunogen (Fig. 56) which occurs naturally on Melos; it is a renewable source which would have been easy to harvest. Soluble impurities could probably have been removed locally from fumarolic alum by redissolving and reprecipitating the material to produce aluminium-sulphate rich powder. We think this could have taken place at the archaeological site of Aghia Kyriaki (Fig. 57) (Photos-Jones and Hall *in press*), but it has proved very difficult to find definitive evidence mainly because the waste materials would be easily assimilated into the environment; there is abundant pottery, in the shape of *lekanae,* open, large diameter shallow vessels, which suggest large-scale industrial applications, as well as storage (*pithoi*) and transport (*amphorae*) vessels. Aghia Kyriaki and neighbouring Paleochori have at some stage in the history of the settlements been buried under sediments. The results of analysis of sediments from within vessels are rather undiagnostic of the original contents of the container since this area of SE Melos is hydrothermally active, and so the soil cannot be readily distinguished from the minerals one is seeking to investigate.

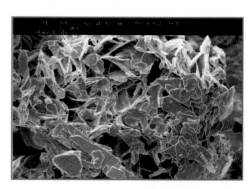

Fig. 56 *SEM image of fumarolic alunogen from the Aghia Kyriaki solfatara. Scale bar:200 microns.*

The first mention of sulphur (Greek *theion*) as a disinfectant is presented in Homer when Odysseus asks his old nurse to bring him sulphur to disinfect the halls of his palace after the killing of his wife's suitors (*Odyssey* 22.483; 22.495). Apart from fumigant, sulphur had many uses: fuel for burning, a source of light, fulling as a bleach in wool preparation, and a medicine (Pliny *Nat. Hist.* XXXV.174-7). Traditional therapeutic uses included as a powder in ointment for skin complaints, a mild laxative, fumes for the relief of coughs and mucus in lungs, and in a bath for rheumatism. Also when burnt in air, it formed a powerful disinfectant for contagious diseases.

Melos has been a sulphur-producing island *par excellence* and the archaeological evidence for the exploitation of sulphur in Melos is presented elsewhere (Photos-Jones and Hall *in press*); there are essentially two types of mineralisation, deep vein sulphur and sulphur growing in association with

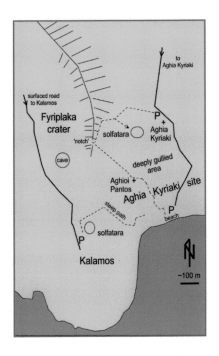

Fig. 57 *(left)* Map of the Aghia Kyriaki area showing current access to Kalamos and the solfatara of Aghia Kyriaki.

Fig. 58 *(right)* View of the Kalamos peninsula, looking SW over the bay and archaeological site of Aghia Kyriaki.

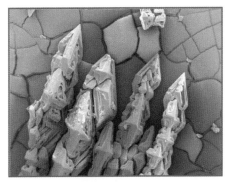

Fig. 59 *(left)* Sulphur collection at Kalamos. **Fig. 60** *(right)* SEM image of sulphur grains from Kalamos; each grain is approximately 1mm long.

alunogen in the Melian solfataras. In SE Melos one can visit two solfataras: one is very active and located at Kalamos with sulphurous vapour emitted from rock orifices (Figs. 59 and 60), and a second now largely quiet near the chapel of Aghia Kyriaki (Figs. 55 and 57). The easiest way to reach the solfatara of Aghia Kyriaki is to park at the chapel of Aghia Kyriaki and walk west skirting the cultivated fields before alunogen in the Melian solfataras.

To access the Fyriplaka crater and Kalamos, continue west through the 'notch' in the Fyriplaka crater rim. There was formerly a substantial track through the 'notch' but this is rapidly being eroded away. From the beach at Aghia Kyriaki there are two possible routes (Fig. 57) to reach Kalamos (Fig. 58). There was a substantial track up to the chapel of Aghioi Pantes and to the 'notch' but this only exists now in part due to erosion. The second route is eastwards up a steep footpath that is still passable and would have provided more direct access to Kalamos at the time of occupation and use of the Aghia Kyriaki site. If one wishes to avoid completely Aghia Kyriaki, Kalamos can now be reached conveniently from the north and the main part of the island via a modern tarmac road that runs through the centre of Fyriplaka crater.

Minor earths

Ambelitis

The earliest reference to *ambelitis* is in Theophrastus (*On Stones* 85); without naming it specifically he mentions an earth from Cilicia which becomes glutinous/colloidal when boiled and is applied to vines. Dioscorides (*De Materia Medica* V.181) says that some call it *pharmakitis*. It also comes from Seleukia in Syria, so it is possible that the two authors might be talking about the same place. Dioscorides mentions that contrary to other earths it is black, dissolves in oil and was used for dyeing hair. It is difficult to conceive of an argillaceous earth that is that black - no organic-rich mudstones are so black. Pliny (*Nat. Hist.* XXXV.167) mentions other lesser known earths, Knidos, Kassandra and Kyzicos being examples. There are also earths to be found between Oropos and Aulis in Attica which are compared with that of Potuoli (Pozzuoli) and are thought to be pozzolanas on account of their hydraulic properties since they harden upon contact with water. Pozzuoli in the Bay of Naples gave its name to pozzolana: volcanic tuff which has cementaceous properties and contributes to making lime-based cement a 'hydraulic cement' that can set under water. This type of cement was used by the Romans, and volcanic rock that is added to cement to make it hydraulic is still called pozzolana. In the Aegean, Melos is currently (2011) a major source and Santorini was formerly.

Pnigitis Earth or *Terra Pnigitis*

Pnigitis occurs in large quantities and is glutinous. It has the same properties as Eretria Earth but is not as good (Dioscorides V.177; Pliny *Nat. Hist.* XXXV.194). Since it is similar to the Eretrian Earth its colour is white and grey, yet Galen (*De Materia Medica* IX.4) and Paul of Aegina regard it as black. According to Agricola (*De Re Fossilium*) its source is Libya, but it is most likely that it came from the word *pnigo* meaning to choke on account of its sticky properties upon swallowing.

Silenusian Earth or *Terra Selinusiae*

It is not clear whether this earth come from Selinous in Sicily or Selinous in Cilicia. First noted by Dioscorides (V.175), Pliny (*Nat. Hist.* XXXV.194) says that it has a milky colour and dissolves easily in water.

Tymphaic gypsum

Theophrastus (*On Stones* LXIV.67) mentions that Tymphaic gypsum was used for the whitening of clothes and occasionally by painters. Pliny places Tymphaia in Aetolia (*Nat. Hist.* XXXIV.6) and in Macedonia (*Nat. Hist.* XXXIV.35) (Levidis 1994, 482).

Belon's scepticism

Mineral enrichment as ritual

Having surveyed the localities of many of the earths can we at least establish the composition of one of them, namely Lemnian Earth? Even from the last part of the 19th century there have been a number of attempts to analyse it. Dana's Mineralogy of the late 19th century refers to the mineral sphragidite (an alumino-silicate of sodium) as one originating *".... from Stalimene, the ancient Lemnos. It was also called terra sigillata. It was dug for medicinal purposes once a year, cut into spindle-shaped pieces and stamped with a seal, and hence the name sigillata in Latin and sphragis in Greek"* (Palache *et al.* 1944).

Fig. 61a *Detail of Fig. 7 showing Lemnian Earth being loaded on to boats in a harbour.*

Alfred Philippson undertook a mineralogical study of Lemnian Earth and was rather puzzled: *"The sample is an altered (?) clay which consists of small angular fragments of quartz, clay, iron oxide and a brownish substance which I cannot identify; what I can say is that it is not hornblende. I cannot draw any final conclusions regarding the original clayey rock. In any case, it is not volcanic rock. I cannot observe anything particular regarding its usage"* (Tourptsoglou-Stephanidou 1986, 562).

Two additional sets of chemical analyses were produced by Daubeny and De Launay (Tourptsoglou-Stephanidou 1986, 454, 506), but neither was particularly revealing as to the nature of the material and its usefulness as a medicine. However, the analyses suggest the presence of aluminium-silicate clay, possibly with sodium and calcium, which would point to the presence of one or more montmorillonite group minerals. It is unfortunate that potash is not mentioned, because confirmation of a lack of potash, which is present in the common clay illite, would be a further indication of montmorillonite. The high iron content suggests the presence of an iron oxide or oxyhydroxide component, probably hematite, in keeping with a reddish colour.

In brief, the analyses are consistent with the results of Dana's Mineralogy regarding the mineral sphragidite. From the above, it can be concluded that the evidence at the time was that Lemnian Earth was simply a clay, hence Luis de Launay's statement at the introduction to this book (Launay 1895, 16) registering his frustration at not being able to pinpoint the active ingre-dient. It is possible that Lemnian Earth acted as a placebo, that is, a phar-macologically inert substance with its efficacy relying on the attitude, both cognitive and behavioural, of the person involved. But it is also the case that the active ingredient responsible for its curative properties requires a more complex methodology in its scientific detection notwithstanding the possibility that an ordinary clay poultice might act as a 'medicine' simply by decreasing inflammation and swelling. We consider that there was no organic component in the pellet; had that been the case Galen would not have been able to take to Rome all these thousands of tablets.

Fig. 61b *Detail of Fig. 7 showing procession to the site of the Lemnian Earth working (shown as a round 'pit' in the centre of the field).*

We turn now to the ritual of the extraction of Lemnian Earth as described by Galen who was present on the day and presumably at the site. The ritual itself has fascinated many travellers since Galen's visit since it addresses many issues ranging from the exact location and actual digging of the pit, the religious pageantry, the Earth's presumed enrichment by washing, to the sealing and distribution of the material. All these events would have taken place in a time span of less than 24 hours, and the totality and speed of their execution must have been so well rehearsed that the critical details eluded even the most astute of observers. The ritual of the preparation of the Lemnian *sphragis* is described by Galen as follows:

"The priestess collects this, to the accompaniment of some local ceremony, no animals being sacrificed, but wheat and barley being given back to the land in exchange. She then takes it to the city, mixes it with water so as to make moist mud, shakes this violently and then allows it to stand. Thereafter she removes first the superficial water, and next the greasy part of the earth below this, leaving only the stony and sandy part at the bottom, which is useless. She now dries the greasy mud until it reaches the consistency of soft wax. Of this she takes small portions and imprints upon them the seal of Artemis namely the goat, then again she dries these in the shade till they are absolutely free from moisture." Galen continues to explain that the priestess, after filling a *"whole wagon with earth, this she took into the town, as I have said, and from it prepared the far-famed Lemnian seals."*(Galen in Brock 1929, 192).

Belon also describes the ritual of its extraction. The day's events were preceded by a religious service at the chapel of Aghios Sotiras (St Saviour). The Turkish governor of the island, Turkish and Greek notables, as well as some priests and monks, took part in the ceremony. The digging began at or before sunrise and continued for six hours, after which the pit was closed and left undisturbed until the next year. Some Lemnian Earth was given to the officers present and other bystanders, but the bulk of it was sent to the Sultan in Constantinople. A certain amount was sold on the spot by the local magistrate to local merchants.

There can now be little doubt that the extraction of Lemnian Earth witnessed by both Galen and Belon took place around a pit. Yet some travellers' accounts make it clear that at the extraction site there was both a pit from which the Earth was extracted and a spring, whose function is less clear. In an attempt to scrutinize the events of the day of the extraction, we focus our attention on the relationship between the pit and the spring.

In reference to the pit, the Dutchman, Joos van Ghistele, who visited Lemnos in 1485 reported that: "*(Terra Sigillata) is produced in Lemnos in a pool which dries up every summer and is full of water in winter. When this pool begins to dry up, a thick scum, variegated in colour, forms on its surface. This is skimmed off and laid on clean planks as required, according to the method in use locally. When dry, it is made up into round pellets or flat cakes*". It has been pointed out that the Dutch/Flemish word for scum is equivalent to "*a scum on the surface of beer or wine caused by fungus*" (Hasluck and Hasluck 1929, 674).

The 'frothiness' of Lemnian Earth in the Dutchman's account also brings to focus another account of Sibthorp who reported that "*the 'sacred earth' springs out by itself*". Figure 62 illustrates schematically the process of enrichment according to the Dutchman's account. It 'jumps' and 'overflows' are the expressions used (Covel in Tourptsoglou-Stephanidou 1986, 161, and Sibthorp in Tourptsoglou-Stephanidou 1986, 450). A similar eyewitness account of 'bubbling earth' was given by a Kotsinas potter in the late 1970s to Psaropoulou (1986, 237).

Jacopo Salerno, emissary of Venice to the Sultan in 1581, gave the following account of the extraction activities: "*On a hillock there is a spring; its water is directed through a channel to a pit which has formed naturally (by the accumulating water) ..... the pit is covered with planks cut and joined together like the cover for a box which they lock with a key.*" On the prescribed day (6th of August), "*....they change the course of the water, so that it does not run towards the pit. They lift the cover and remove very carefully all the overlying water (in the pit), which they collect in buckets and (eventually) with sponges. Then they dig the mud and sort the best quality of earth out first. Then they dig another type of earth, not as good and then a third. With these three varieties of earth they make three different types of pellets as well as cups for drinking water; they seal them with the stamp of the Grand Efendi, and they fire them all to become hard*" (Salerno in Tourptsoglou-Stephanidou 1986, 119*)*.

Another detailed account of the extraction and processing of Lemnian Earth was given by Covel (in Tourptsoglou-Stephanidou 1986, 193) and in Bent (1893) based on his visit to Lemnos about 1677. Covel was evidently aware of the earlier account of Belon and also mentions that Lemnian Earth is recovered by digging close to the east side of a spring: "*On the east side of the spring within a foot of my hand's breadth of it they every year take out the earth on the 6th of August about three hours after sunrise..... Thus they take it out: before day they begin and digge a well about 1.5 yards wide and a little above a man's height deep. ....and then the earth is taken out soft and loomy, some of it like butter which the Greeks say and*

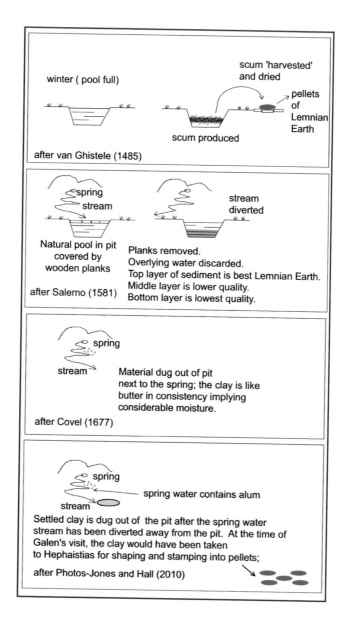

Fig. 62 *The drawing illustrates schematically the accounts of Ghistele and Salerno (in Tourptsoglou-Stefanidou 1986) and of Covel (in 1677) of the process of enrichment. Our interpretation of the procedure at the time of Galen is also shown. The pit and spring are related in that the spring is seen not merely as a landmark for the location of the pit, but rather as an integral part of the process of natural and artificial enrichment taking place over the course of the year. Had Lemnian earth been extracted more than once in the year, its efficacy may have been compromised. All references to travelers' accounts in Tourptsoglou-Stephanidou 1986).*

the Turks believe is turned out of rocky stone into soft clay by virtues of their mass. when they have taken out 20-30 kintals of the Greeks use they fill it up again and so leave it stop't without any guard in the world" (Bent 1893, 284).

The spring appears to be clear excellent water at first, but on *"falling down a little lower, looseth its water in a kind of milky bogge"*. Covel witnessed the processing of Lemnian Earth at a large fountain in Hagiapate or Aghios Ypatios (Tourptsoglou-Stephanidou 1986, 161); this was a Turkish village where the authorities had the right to take some Lemnian Earth and give it to local potters to make pots:

"They first dissolve (sic) it in water, well working it with their hands; then let the water pass through a sive (sic), and what remains they throw away. They let the water stand till settled, then take of (sic) the clear, and when dry enough, they mould in their hands; and most of this we have is shaped from thence. It is all here white, yet I had some given me flesh-coloured. I enquired diligently about it, and they all told me it came out of the same pit; but I expect some of these fellows have found some other place which they conceal."

Figure 62 illustrates schematically the process of enrichment according to different accounts. Based on these descriptions provided above we suggest that there was a spring in the immediate vicinity of the pit from which the Earth was extracted. The water passed the pit into which it was allowed to drain during the course of a whole year. Sediments within the pit were then allowed to settle, and clay, silt and sand to separate. It is the fine levigated clay that would make up the medicinal Earth which would be removed at source and would require no further treatment. Galen (*On Simple Drugs* XIII.249) makes it clear that Lemnian Earth should not be washed more than once and only the lower grades (non-medicinal) were amenable to further washing: *"...τινές δέ δίς ή τρίς δέονται πλυθήναι.τήν μέν ούν Λημνίαν έτοίμην λαμβάνεις άπαξ πεπλυμένην υπό τής ιερείας, εκ δευτέρου δε πλυθήναι μή δεομένην"* [Some (earths) are washed twice or three times; but the Lemnian Earth you receive ready washed only once by the priestess; it is not advisable to wash it a second time] (author's translation). This comment suggests that the medicinal Lemnian Earth contained a soluble component. Further washing would dilute Lemnian Earth and reduce its efficacy. Thus at the time of Galen, whatever washing took place was not of Lemnian Earth the medicine, but its lower grades. Given the present arrangement at the Phtheleidia spring, it is difficult to see how the place of extraction could lie above the present outlet (trough in Fig. 18) of the spring. So we suggest that at the time it may have been tapped further uphill.

Belon discusses two springs in the vicinity of the pit, Covel only one but Albacario, a Spanish ambassador to the Ottoman Court (in Tourptsoglou-Stephanidou 1986, 175), clearly mentions three springs, the largest being close to the *Sotiras* chapel and running into the nearby field. He also states that Lemnian Earth is mostly white to pinkish, rarely yellow to red. Finally, De Launay suggests that Lemnian Earth was obtained from the immediate vicinity of the spring, after the waters were diverted (De Launay in Tourptsoglou-Stephanidou 1986, 464-507). We suggest that had Lemnian earth been extracted more than once in the year, its efficacity may have been severely compromised.

Belon's scepticism addressed?

A recipe for Lemnian Earth

Lemnian Earth could not have been a single mineral but rather a combination of inorganic minerals. These minerals were introduced both naturally and artificially through an enrichment mechanism. The bulk composition of Lemnian Earth, the medicine, was essentially a clay consisting of approximately, montmorillonite, kaolin, alum and hematite. This rather speculative answer which gives essentially a 'recipe' for the medicinal Lemnian Earth needs to be justified and explained; it is summarised below following a fuller account already given in Hall and Photos-Jones (2008).

The case for montmorillonite

Documentary evidence: Galen mentions that one of the three varieties of Lemnian Earth was used for washing cloth. We know that the cleansing properties of the clay, montmorillonite led to its use by fullers (Robertson 1986, 7–10). We can therefore infer that Lemnian Earth contained the clay, montmorillonite. Galen also describes how Lemnian Earth was shaped into small tablets and stamped with a goat motif. Montmorillonite improves plasticity in clay (Smoot 1963) and thus the presence of at least some montmorillonite in Lemnian Earth would benefit the production of such tablets.

Field evidence for montmorillonite: Montmorillonite was found in a sample of volcanic rock in the vicinity of the Phthelidia spring and was identified using powder XRD. Montmorillonite is a common alteration product of volcanic rocks. Outcropping volcanic rocks are present in the crags behind the spring. Even the presence of a small amount of montmorillonite in a rock sample indicates that there is the potential for montmorillonite-rich rocks somewhere in the vicinity. This is because montmorillonite can be produced by a hydrothermal alteration process (hot water permeating through the rock) which has to be more intense in some places to produce larger amounts of the clay. Indeed, fine silt accumulating near the edge of a track proved, on XRD analysis, to be rich in expanding clay further confirming the potential presence of concentrations of montmorillonite-type expanding (absorbing) clays in this area.

Estimated montmorillonite content: How much montmorillonite was present? Montmorillonite could not have been the sole constituent as the tablets would be prone to excessive shrinkage on drying out. An estimated *c.* 40% of the total is suggested.

The case for kaolin

Documentary evidence: The documentary accounts do not provide any evidence for the presence of kaolin other than the observation that Lemnian Earth was fine-grained and earthy, and that its colour was variable. As kaolin is white, it would have contributed to making the often reddish Lemnian Earth pinkish or flesh coloured (Bent 1893, 284). Reports do indicate a variable colour of Lemnian Earth.

Field evidence for kaolin: We detected kaolin (or at least a 7 Å clay which is most likely to be kaolin) in analysed (XRD) samples of altered volcanic rock taken from close to the Phthelidia spring. Kaolin is anticipated to be present in such altered volcanic rocks. This alteration may be due to weathering but can also result from hydrothermal alteration. The altered rocks will usually become whiter as kaolin is formed.
Estimated kaolin content: 35%

The case for alum

Documentary evidence for alum:
Galen suggested that Lemnian Earth was astringent. While the description is sometimes applied to other materials such as clays which can be dessicants, we consider that comments by Galen provide powerful evidence that alum was a significant component of Lemnian Earth. We also take into account Galen's statement that Lemnian Earth should not be washed more than once. Alum is very soluble and, although potentially absorbed by the clays present, it seems inevitable that excessive washing would remove it.

97

The astringent nature of Lemnian Earth is also mentioned by Pomet in his early 18th century *History of drugs* and by Charas, the late 17th century French author of the *Royal Pharmacopoeia* (in Thompson 1914, 440) but we prefer to place more weight on Galen's statement. Alum is therefore considered to be the active ingredient.

Field evidence for alum: We did not find actual alum in samples recovered from the Phthelidia spring area but the presence of alunite was the main clue indicating that alum could have been produced in this geological setting (Photos-Jones *et al.* 2000). Alunite is an insoluble potassium aluminium sulphate mineral similar in composition to alum. It is quite rare and forms on relatively high temperature hydrothermal acid sulphate alteration of volcanic rocks. Alunite is often found associated with alum group minerals and native sulphur, as on Melos (see section on Melian Earth). Its presence in rocks in the Phthelidia spring area therefore indicates that the hydrothermal processes in this area had the potential to produce alum-group minerals. This alteration process is explained in detail above in relation to the origin of white altered rock on Melos.

Even if it had formed in abundance, alum is unlikely to be found in surface outcrops near the Phthelidia spring because the geothermal process is no longer active and, being very soluble, alum would have long ago been washed out of surface rocks by rainwater. The samples recovered show pronounced alteration reflected in their variable colour. We infer that the different 'varieties' of Lemnian Earth with various textures (sticky, greasy and granular) and colours (white, yellow and red) that are referred to in the texts are products of hydrothermal alteration, with various proportions of the alteration products. Such hydrothermal alteration is not unexpected in the proximity of a geological fault in a former volcanic area. This fault is inferred from the linear outcrop of crags of volcanic rock at Phthelidia (Fig. 19) and presumably also constituted the main focus for the former hydrothermal solutions. Altered and weathered pyroclastic rock was observed in the crags about 20 m NW of the Phthelidia spring (Figs. 16 and 19). The rock here is grey and slightly weathered but is distinctly reddish in places, for example along joint surfaces, consistent with hydrothermal alteration. The existence of alunite in the rock samples collected is therefore only an indicator of the former potential presence of alum.

The deposits of altered rock could have been worked as described by Belon in 'vein-like' features, presumably located at geological faults and fracture zones. Over time, soluble sulphates such as alum would have been 'washed' by rain out of the high ground of altered volcanic rocks, into the alluvial sediment of the area of the fields close to the spring (Fig. 19). They could therefore have found their way into man-made traps (pits) set in place and worked by ritual, such as that described by Hasluck (1909-10, 226) and Salerno (in Tourptsoglou-Stephanidou 1986, 119 n. 7) in the accounts given above. Thus alum could have been concentrated by absorption by clay minerals as they settled out of the spring water over the period of a year.

Estimated alum content: c. 20%. It is likely that the alum content is controlled by the absorption of alum on to montmorillonite (Hall and Photos-Jones 2008).

The case for hematite

Documentary evidence: Theophrastus, Dioscorides and Pliny refer to Lemnian *miltos* indicating that it was red and, as well as naming it *Terra Lemnia* or *Terra Sigillata*, Pliny refers to it as *Terra Rubricata* (*Nat. Hist.* XXXV.14). It is his word '*rubrica*' in relation to Lemnian Earth that clearly implies that it was red. Galen also uses the name Lemnian *miltos*, adding that *it differs from this* [i.e. *miltos*] *in not leaving a stain when handled* (Galen XIII.246b; in Brock 1929, 192). We can therefore infer that the early medicinal Lemnian Earth did contain sufficient colorant to make it distinctly red. However, later travellers to Lemnos (to the lands of the Ottoman empire) clearly state that the Earth was yellow (Agricola 1530, 215). Belon mentions that the Turks differentiated two types of earth, the *thin-i makhtoum-i ahmer* - the red earth - and the *thin-i makhtoum-i ebiez*, the white earth, the latter considered of lower quality (in Tourptsoglou-Stephanidou 1986, 111 n. 4). The most likely natural agent that could give a red colour to Lemnian Earth, as in the case of Keian *Miltos*, is fine-grained hematite. Although cinnabar, HgS, is a potential candidate there is no good geological case nor clues from the literary accounts. Our fieldwork indicated that red soil and red sediments are rare in north-eastern Lemnos, but we did note concentrations of red clay within the archaeological site of Hephaistias.

Field evidence for hematite: Local soils are certainly susceptible to reddening on heating; for example, we observed distinctly reddened soils in areas where grass and scrub had been burnt recently. However, red Lemnian Earth is unlikely to have been produced by artificial heating of local brown (limonitic) clay. Reddening of rocks along surfaces and joints in the vicinity of the Phthelidia spring is taken as evidence of hydrothermal alteration (Hall and Photos-Jones 2008).

Medicinal Properties of Hematite: Hematite is inert and has no significant properties in relation to medicines although iron is known to be a require-

99

ment of good health. Iron is at the root of metabolism in all life forms and the biochemical mechanism of blood. The ferric iron that is in hematite is relatively insoluble. Medicinal red iron springs are well known in many cultures, for instance the Scottish Highlands folklore relating to healing practices abound with reference to them (Photos-Jones *et al.* 1998); blacksmiths were healers in remote highland communities. Trace iron is typically provided in medicines in ferrous salts such as ferrous sulphate (Sweetman 2007). In a recent study on iron oxides Tran *et al.* (2010) have shown that nanoparticles of Fe-oxide (magnetite) have bactericidal properties against *Staphilococcus aureus*, while at the same time increasing growth of human bone cells.

Estimated hematite content: *c.* 5%. The concentration of fine hematite required to give a reddish colour to Lemnian Earth is unlikely to have exceeded that amount.

In conclusion, Lemnian Earth consisted essentially of smectitic clays enriched in aluminium sulphate salts. The bulk composition of Lemnian Earth, the medicine, was essentially a clay consisting of approximately 40% montmorillonite, 35% kaolin, 20% alum and 5% hematite. The variety of Lemnian Earth with medicinal properties was red in colour, at least in antiquity, fine grained and could be stamped and transported as tablets which were round and air-dried rather than baked by heating in a kiln. It must have been greasy, palatable and hence soft and probably soluble, at least in part, on moistening. It had a pleasant taste of unknown origin.

The pit would have provided a means for concentrating both clay and soluble minerals. A soluble component of alluvial clay like alum would be expected to be rather elusive and would not necessarily be present in present-day near-surface soils and sediments. The pit was not simply an open-cast working to provide clay but an integral part of the enrichment process that involved the collection of both clays and soluble minerals. This explains the ritual associated with its opening.

Recently, a different composition for Lemnian Earth has been offered (Mottana 2006): montmorillonite and illite with a mineral that is intermediate between alunite and jarosite responsible for Lemnian Earth's weathered purple-red colour, astringency and curative properties. Unfortunately the author does not give any reference for his information and nothing to support his opinion. Nevertheless, Mottana (2006) plots an interesting historical trajectory of the interest in stones as opposed to herbs and roots as medicinal substances, firstly as curiosities and increasingly as medicines on their own or mixed with herbs or animal products. This upward trajectory continued until the early Renaissance. Then the trajectory took a downward trend and degenerated into alchemy; however, he now argues, modern pharmacological studies into mineral-based antibiotics is certainly set to reverse this trend.

We raise two additional issues here: the *ayiochoma* - sacred Earth - and the *ayiasma* - sacred water - represent the two end members of the same 'medicine'. It may be that the holy water was a later introduction, part of a Christian ritual rather than a pagan one, or even the re-interpretation of the pagan ritual of washing of the Earth, by the church. It is not possible to tell, but their proximity to each other cannot be disregarded. It is also possible that the Phtheloudia spring fed the spring of the *ayiochoma*. In other words, the waters of the former were redirected prior to the construction of the castle of Kotsinos to provide water for the community within its walls. The second issue is a more nagging one. Why are the classical sources rather 'casual' regarding mineral-based medicines and why are they not 'ready' to separate them from pigments and washing powders? *Theriacs* and *alexipharmaka*, albeit plant-based, certainly are treated at an elevated status compared to other *pharmaka*; furthermore, it has to be acknowledged that the global tradition started by early *roizotomoi* and *pharmakides*, namely looking to nature for healing continues unabated if not with renewed force to this very day.

But earths? Is the message that underwrites the classical authors' treatment of these substances one of scepticism? Or is it that they viewed these materials as essentially purveyors of well-being *via* 'cleanliness' and as a means of complying with the message of the Hippocratic belief in the balance of humours (hot and cold, wet and dry) within (and outwith) the body? Perhaps these authors were simply baffled as to why these materials were effective, so they simply ignored further questions; pigments, washing powders and medicines were ultimately materials with clearly discernible and describable properties. If there were ever to be a hypothetical chance encounter in the afterlife, one would hate to be on the receiving end of a rather dismissive look by Pliny, let alone Galen, assuming one plucked enough courage to ask them that question!

Summary of results of investigation: Our geological prospection in the NE of the island, the area associated with the extraction of Lemnian Earth, prompted us to re-examine the myths and rituals associated with the properties usages and extraction of Lemnian Earth. In our original article (Hall and Photos-Jones 2008) we took the stance that if scientific enquiry had so far failed to detect the active ingredient, it was possible that the problem may lie with the methodology of the scientific enquiry rather than the limitations of Lemnian Earth as a medicine. Pivotal to the investigation became the ritual of its extraction.

Where did it take place? It is almost certain that the locality of its extraction, both in antiquity and the post-medieval period, was in the vicinity of the Phthelidia spring. This is certainly a strong candidate for a Lemnian Earth locality on account of the local hydrothermally altered rocks.

What exactly was being extracted and how? Since the extraction ritual was happening in a rather charged atmosphere and over a period of a few hours once a year, it was expected that even the keenest of observers might have missed critical stages leading to the event and subsequent to it. One omission seemed to us to be the association of the pit, the focus of the activities on the day, and the water which appeared to have been directed over it over the course of a whole year. Also of concern has been the issue of washing or further processing, after extraction. Why was that necessary, and for what grades of Lemnian Earth, given that there was clearly more than one grade?

Therefore the water became the focus of our investigation. Could the water source enrich the clay-rich pit with soluble salts originating from the underlying volcanic rocks? And what are the salts? Analyses of samples of rocks and sediments led to the identification of alunite, a pointer to alum, within altered volcanic rock. Astringent alum's properties as a medicine were known in antiquity but to our knowledge it is not clear why it was effective. Modern pharmacology does not seem to consider it a research priority presumably because of the existence of much more potent alternative medication.

Throughout antiquity, 'death by poisoning' must have been paramount in the minds of the people and any potential antidote to poison was much sought. Today similar fears are less prominent, although dysentery as a result of drinking polluted water is still an important issue in the developing world. Both Dioscorides and Galen make it quite clear that Lemnian Earth was an effective medicine against dysentery. We highlight the evidence that alum as astringent and bactericide was the most likely active ingredient in Lemnian Earth and propose how alum got there in the first place. However, how and why it worked lies beyond the scope of this presentation, and besides current research shows that some clays may be potent bactericides in their own right.

We now consider the issue of the soluble alum as an ingredient of the spring water, as opposed to the insoluble alunite which is part of the rocks over which the water runs. If alum was dissolved in the spring water then the medicinal properties really lie with the water. From that we can infer that the application of clay rich in alum was in practical and psychological terms a more effective medicine given the anti-swelling properties of clays. We are therefore faced with the possibility that the emphasis of the investigation should have shifted from the clay to the water of that particular spring; furthermore, that the clay pits into which the water collects is really the vessel for concentration as well as the vehicle for the key ingredient, i.e. the alum.

A further point to consider is the issue of evaporation. For alum to concentrate into the absorbent clay, evaporation would presumably be advantageous. This means that the pit would have to have been left open or partly open, yet this is in contradiction to the pit 'bubbling'. The origin of this event described by eye-witness accounts may be a gaseous evolution due to bacterial activity or a deeper sourced gas. The latter cannot be discarded, especially in consideration of the evidence for faulting and hydrothermal alteration of rocks in the vicinity.

The volcanic-related events of the island as exemplified by hydrothermal energy rather than volcanic eruption brings us back 'full cycle' to Hephaistos and the shaping of his identity with respect to Lemnos and *vice versa*. Lemnian Earth forms an integral part of the myths associated with Lemnos which essentially start with the fall of Hephaistos on the island. He is the 'reason' behind volcanic activity and the islanders' acquaintance with metallurgy at the Bronze Age settlement at Poliochni. His conjugal misadventures were the cause of the first Lemnian crime which has been associated with the Argonauts, and in order to justify the Mycenaean settlement of the island. Also there are the various versions of the myths of Philoctetes' sufferings while on Lemnos. The subsequent settlement of Lemnos by the Pelasgians forms the basis of the second Lemnian crime. Philostratus in the 3rd century AD, in recalling the nine-day festival commemorating the events of the first Lemnian crime, clearly shows that the two sets of myths were well integrated.

Geological prospection for Lemnian Earth, its chemical analysis and the scrutiny of its chemical and physical properties can bear results only when fitted within a larger framework of documentary and archaeological evidence as well as the mythological background relevant to this material. We suggest that myths and rituals can be 'records' of geological, environmental and anthropogenic events which survive scientific scrutiny. In other words, they can provide a firm base for scientific enquiry. It is on account of this proposal, and the working hypothesis that Lemnian Earth was an expanding smectitic clay (probably montmorillonite) containing a soluble aluminous sulphate salt responsible for its medicinal properties, that we feel justified in suggesting that "the *application of chemistry to myths can be carried out with no 'risks' so long as it is appreciated that the 'myth' represents the whole and the 'chemistry' a part thereof*".

Concluding Remarks

We return now to the questions posed at the start of the book. Can Lemnian Earth exist outside the documentary record? We believe that in principle it can. The geology of the north of Lemnos in the area around the Phtheleidia spring has begun to be closely investigated and samples have been retrieved for analyses. Underpinning the production of Lemnian Earth was the ritual of its extraction. Did Galen's and Pierre Belon's accounts, written fourteen centuries apart, refer to the same location? We suggest that Galen and Belon, although starting from two different points, did arrive at the same place. What were the main characteristics of the place of extraction? A pit from where the Earth was extracted and a spring or perhaps two 'springs'. One needs to be careful in the way a 'spring' is defined - is it natural or is it man-made, as most accounts are very specific about the pit but rather vague about the spring and the role it played. References to the washing of the Earth *after* it was extracted have 'clouded' the role of the spring water. We argued that this role is paramount in generating the product itself and that subsequent washing must have been unnecessary since that would have reduced the efficacy of the Earth by dissolving soluble components like alum away, and thus reducing astringency. Washing of Lemnian Earth at Aghia Hypati was probably aimed at enriching the lower grades. It was the diverted spring water that brought the main ingredient, dissolved alum, to the clay pit; this could only have happened *via* a deliberate process carried out during the course of the year when all attention was drawn away from the site. This 'detail' could have been known only to a select few, but it did not escape the observant eye of some eye-witnesses.

So perhaps Lemnian Earth, the raw material, can only turn into Lemnian Earth, the medicine, in the present day if all of the above steps are reproduced accurately and under controlled conditions; assuming they can be reproduced, the products will need to be monitored by sampling and analysis. The study of the geology of the area and the proposed composition of Lemnian Earth constitutes only the first steps in the possible 'reinstatement' of the Earth as a medicinal clay. Apart from the properties of montmorillonite and kaolin, what precisely is the role of alum and or indeed very fine hematite? Again there is a need for testing under controlled laboratory conditions. As for Samian Earth, this presents another challenge: what is the role of boron and borates within the montmorillonite clay assuming that boron was the active ingredient in *collyrium*? Most science-based investigators since Theophrastus, Dioscorides and Pliny have opted for the chemical characterization of an earth according to a specific clay mineral. What field work has shown is that they are more likely to be composite materials since very few natural materials are likely to be pure. To say that it is a composite material means that there is more than one major component that is influencing the properties of the artefact, medicine or pigment. Furthermore a medicinal active ingredient might be present in a very low concentration, rendering issues of relative amounts of less importance. Indeed the further study of the nature and properties of Lemnian Earth may usher a new perspective in *geophagia* and the relationship between complex minerals and clay-based substances, bacteria, animal behaviour and the promotion of human health and well-being.

It is now perhaps appropriate to return to De Launay's comment laid out at the start of this book about the *'application of chemistry to myths'* and its (chemistry's) failure to resolve them. De Launay (1895) was right: chemical analysis alone would never resolve the 'myth'. Chemical analysis of mineral substances delivers data on composition while the monitoring and measurement of physical and chemical parameters addresses issues of nature and properties. Surely between composition, nature and properties, one can build a pretty accurate understanding of the 'myth'. But beyond composition and properties of materials lies the vast and largely unquantifiable 'universe' of beliefs about health and well-being and the ever-burning desire in human nature to achieve and maintain both; this desire to be and feel well - unquantifiable by physical units of measurement - is familiar to medical practitioners and even life-style gurus but is beyond the scope of most natural scientists; yet it is the missing parameter in the resolution of the 'myth'.

105

References

Agricola G, *De Re Metallica*. Translated from the first Latin edition of 1556 by Herbert Clark Hoover and Lou Henry Hoover. *The Mining Magazine*, Salisbury House, London, 1912.

Agricola G, *De Natura Fossilium* (Textbook on Mineralogy). Translated from the first Latin edition of 1546 by Mark Chance Bandy and Jean A. Bandy. The Geological Society of America, New York, 1955.

Agricola G, 1530, *Bernanus*.

Bailey KC, 1929, *The Elder Pliny's Chapters on Chemical Subjects. Part I*. London: Arnold.

Bailey KC, 1932, *The Elder Pliny's Chapters on Chemical Subjects. Part II*. London: Arnold.

Bakhuizen SC, 1976, *Chalcis-in-Euboea, Iron and the Chalcidians Abroad*. Leiden: Brill.

Beccaluva L, G Bianchini and M Wilson, 2007, Cenozoic volcanism in the Mediterranean area. Geological Society of America Special Paper 418. Boulder, Colorado.

Beccaluva L, 2007, *Cenozoic volcanism in the Mediterranean area*. Geological Society of America, Boulder, Colorado.

Beck LY, (translator), 2005, *Pedanius Dioscorides of Anazarbus: De materia medica*. Hildesheim: Olms-Weidmann.

Belon PM, 1588, *Les observations de plusieurs singularités et choses memorables trouvées en Grèce*. Paris: Hierosme de Marnes.

Beneke K and G Lagaly, 2002, From Fuller's Earth to Bleaching Earth: A Historical Note. European Clay Group Association Newsletter No.5, 57-78.

Bent JT, 1893, *Early Voyages and Travels in the Levant: I- The diary of Master Thomas Dallam 1599-1600 and II Extracts from the diaries of Dr. John Covel, 1670-1679* (1964 edition). New York: Burt Franklin.

Blake MC, M Bonneau, J Geyssant, JR Kienast, C Lepvrierm, H Maluski and D Papanikolaou, 1981, A geological reconnaissance of the Cycladic blueschist belt, Greece, *Geol. Ass. Amer. Bull.* 92, 247-254.

Boardman J 1967, *Excavations in Chios, 1952-1955: Greek Emporio*. London: British School at Athens and Oxford: Thames and Hudson.

Bostock J and HT Riley, 1855, *The Natural History. Pliny the Elder*. London: Taylor and Francis.

Botz R, D Stuben, G Winckler, R Bayer, M Schmitt and E Faber, 1996, Hydrothermal gases offshore Milos Island, Greece, *Chemical Geology* 130, 161-173.

Brindley GW and G Brown (eds), 1980, *Crystal Structures of Clay Minerals and their X-ray Identification*. London: Mineralogical Society of

Great Britain.

Brock AJ, 1929, *Greek Medicine, being extracts illustrative of medical writers from Hippocrates to Galen*. London: J M Dent and Sons.

Bunnell JE, RB Finkelman, JA Centeno and O Selinus, 2007, Medical Geology: a globally emerging discipline, *Geologica Acta* 5:3, 273-281.

Burandt J, 1994, An Investigation Towards the Identification of Traditional Drawing Inks, *The Book and Paper Group Annual* 13, 9-16.

Bürchner L, 1892, *Das ionische Samos*. Amberg.

Burkert W, 1985, *Greek Religion*. Harvard University Press.

Caley ER and JFC Richards, 1956, *Theophrastus on stones: commentary*. Ohio State University Graduate School Monograph 1. Columbus Ohio.

Cardon D, 2003, *Le Monde des teintures naturelles*. Paris: Belin.

Caskey JL, 1971, Investigations in Keos. Part I: Excavations and Explorations 1966-70, *Hesperia* 40, 359-396.

Caskey JL 1972, Investigations in Keos. Part II: A Conspectus of the Pottery. *Hesperia,* 41, 357-401.

Christidis, G, 1992, Origin, physical and chemical properties of the bentonite deposits from the Aegean Islands of Milos, Kimolos and Chios, Aegean, Greece. Unpublished PhD thesis, University of Leicester.

Christidis GE and PW Scott, 1997, The origin and control of colour of white bentonites from the Aegean islands of Milos and Kimolos, Greece, *Mineralium Deposita* 32, 271-9.

Christidis GE, PW Scott and AC Dunham, 1997, Acid activation and bleaching capacity of bentonites from the islands of Milos and Chios, Aegean, Greece, *Applied Clay Science* 12, 329-347.

Christidis GE, 1998, Comparative study of the mobility of major and trace elements during alteration of an andesite and a rhyolite to bentonite, in the islands of Milos and Kimolos, Aegean, Greece, *Clays and Clay Minerals* 46, 379-399.

Cottier A, 1996, Kean Miltos: The Nature, Composition and Properties of Kean Iron Oxides. Unpublished Undergraduate Dissertation, University of Glasgow.

Da Costa ME, 1757, *A Natural History of Fossils*. London: Davis & Reymers.

Dannenfeldt KH, 1984, The introduction of a new sixteenth-century drug: *Terra Silesiaca, Medical History* 28, 174-188.

De Sélincourt A (trans.), 2003, *The histories / Herodotus; revised with introduction and notes by John Marincola*. London: Penguin Books.

De Simone, C, 1999, *I Tirreni a Lemnos: evidenza linguistica e tradizioni storiche*. Firenze: Olschki.

Dixon JE and AHF Robertson (eds.) 1984, *The Geological Evolution of the Eastern Mediterranean*. London: Geological Society. Blackwell Scientific,

Di Vita A, 1986, Lemno, *Ann. Scuola Archaeologica Atene* LVII-LVIII, 442-491.

Di Vita A, 1988, Lemno, *Ann. Scuola Archaeologica Atene* LXII, 201-208.

Dolan C, 2008, *Hephaistos*, a play written by Chris Dolan, directed by C Bissett, and performed in Glagsow's Oran Mor, February 2008.

Dominy NJ, E Davoust and M Minekus, 2004, Adaptive function of soil consumption: an *in vitro* study modeling the human stomach and small intestine, *J. Experimental Biology* 207, 319-324.

Dotsika E, I Leontiadis, D Poutoukis, R Cioni and B Raco, 2006, Fluid geochemistry of the Chios geothermal area, Chios Island, Greece. *J. Volcanology and Geothermal Research* 154, 237-250.

Eaks IL, 1967, Ripening and astringency removal in persimmon fruits, *Proc Am. Soc. Horticultural Science* 91, 868-875.

Eichholz DE (ed. and transl.), 1962, Pliny the Elder, *Natural History* X: Books 36-37. London and Cambridge Mass.: Loeb.

Eichholz DE, 1965, Theophrastus *De Lapidibus* (*On Stones*) translation and commentary. Oxford: Clarendon Press.

Farella V, 1996, An Inquiry on Philoctetes' disease, *Am. J. Dermatopathol.* 18, 326-329.

Ferrell Jr. RE, 2009, Medicinal clay and spiritual healing, *Clays and Clay Minerals* 56:6, 751-760.

Fragoulis D, E Chaniotakis and MG Stamatakis, 1997, Zeolitic tuffs of Kimolos Island, Aegean Sea, Greece and their industrial potential, *Cement & Concrete Research* 278, 89-905.

Fraser PM, 1969, The Career of Erasistratus of Ceos, *Istituto Lombardo, Rendiconti* 103, 518-537.

Fytikas M, 1989, Updating of the geological and geothermal research on Milos Island, *Geothermics* 18, 485-496.

Fytikas M, F Innocenti, P Manetti, R Mazzuoli, A Peccerillo and LVillari, 1984, Tertiary to Quaternary evolution of volcanism in the Aegean region. In JE Dixon and AHF Robertson (eds.) *The Geological Evolution of the Eastern Mediterranean.* London: Geological Society. Blackwell Scientific, 687-699.

Fytikas MD, 1977, *Geological and geothermal study of Milos. Geological and geophysical Research. XVII.* Athens: Institute of Geology and Mineral Exploration.

Fytikas M and G Vougioukalakis, 1993, Volcanic structure and evolution of Kimolos and Polyegos (Milos island group), *Bull. Geol. Soc. Greece* 28, 221-37. In Greek with English abstract.

Gage J, 1999, *Color and culture: practice and meaning from antiquity to abstraction.* University of California Press.

Galt J, 1813, *Letters from the Levant: containing views of the state of society, manners, opinions, and commerce in Greece and several of the principal islands of the Archipelago.* London: Cadell and Davies.

Garrett DE, 1998, Uses of borates. In DE Garrett (ed.) *Handbook of Deposits, Processing, Properties and Use.* San Diego: Elsevier, 401-29.

Giammatteo M, N Cipriani, L Corona, D Magaldi and G Pantaleoni, 1997, Osservazioni sull'origine e la composizione chimico-mineralogica delle terre sigillate dell'Isola di Samo, *Mineralogia et Petrographica Acta* XL, 327–337.

Gilardi JD, SS Duffey, CA Munn CA and LA Tell, 1999, Biochemical functions of geophagy in parrots: Detoxification of dietary toxins and cytoprotective effects, *J. Chem. Ecol.* 25, 897-922.

Godley AD, 1920, *Herodotus, Histories.* London: Heinemann.

Gombrich EH, 1976, *The Heritage of Apelles.* Oxford: Phaidon Press.

Gunther RT, 1934, *The Greek Herbal of Dioscorides. Illustrated by a Byzantine AD 512, Englished by John Goodyear AD 1655.* Oxford: OUP.

Hall AJ and E Photos-Jones, 2005, The nature of Melian *alumen* and its potential for exploitation in antiquity. In P Borgard, J-P Brun and M Picon (eds.) *L'Alun de Meditérranée. Colloque Int. Naples.* Naples: Centre Jean Bérard, 77–84.

Hall AJ and E Photos-Jones, 2008, Accessing past beliefs and practices: The case of Lemnian Earth, *Archaeometry* 50, 1034-1049.

Hall AJ and E Photos-Jones, 2009, The juice of the pomegranate: quality control for the processing and distribution of *alumen* in antiquity and making sense of Pliny's *Phorimon* and *Paraphoron.* In AJ Shortland, IC Freestone and T Rehren (eds.) *From Mine to Microscope: Advances in the Study of Ancient Technology.* Oxbow: Oxford, 197-206.

Hall AJ, AE Fallick, V Perdikatsis and E Photos-Jones, 2003a, A model for the origin of Al-rich efflorescences near fumaroles, Melos, Greece: enhanced weathering in a geothermal setting, *Mineralogical Magazine* 67, 363-379.

Hall AJ, E Photos-Jones, A McNulty, D Turner and A McRobb, 2003b, Geothermal activity at the archaeological site of Aghia Kyriaki and its significance to Roman industrial mineral exploitation on Melos, Greece, *Geoarchaeology* 18, 333-357.

Harben PW and RL Bates, 1990, *Industrial minerals: geology and world deposits.* London: Metal Bulletin.

Harris E, 2002, Workshop, Marketplace and Household: The Nature of Technical Specialization in Classical Athens and its Influence on Economy and Society. In P Cartledge, EE Cohen and L Foxhall (eds.) *Money, Labour and Land: Approaches to the Economies of Ancient Greece.* London: Routledge, 67-99.

Hasluck FW, 1909-10, Terra Lemnia, *Ann. British School at Athens* 16, 220-231.

Hasluck FW and Hasluck MM, 1929, *Christianity and Islam under the Sultans*. Oxford: OUP.

Haydel SE, CM Remenih and LB Williams, 2008, Broad-spectrum in vitro antibacterial activities of clay minerals against antibiotic-susceptible and antibiotic-resistant bacterial pathogens, *J. Antimicrobial Chemotherapy* 61:2, 353-361.

Healy JF, 1999, *Pliny the Elder on science and technology.* Oxford: OUP.

Heaney S, 1996, *The cure at Troy: a version of Sophocles' Philoctetes.* New York: Farrar, Straus.

Higgins MD and R Higgins, 1996, *A Geological Companion to Greece and the Aegean.* London: Duckworth.

Houston DC, JD Gilardi and AJ Hall, 2001, Soil consumption by Elephants might help minimize the toxic effects of plant secondary compounds in forest browse, *Mammal Review* 31, 249-254.

Hunter JM, OH Horst and RN Thomas, 1989, Religious geophagy as a cottage industry: the holy clay tablet of Esquipulas, Guatemala, *National Geographic Research* 5, 281–295.

Institute of Geology and Mineral Exploration (IGME), 1982, Geological Map of Kea, Athens.

Institute of Geology and Mineral Exploration (IGME), 1993, Geological Map of Greece: 1:50,000 Lemnos Island, Athens.

Jones RE 1986, *Greek & Cypriot Pottery: a review of scientific studies*, Athens. Fitch Laboratory Occasional Paper 1.

Kendall T (ed.), 1996, *Industrial clays: an Industrial Minerals special review.* London: Industrial Minerals Information.

Kritikidis E, 1869, *Τοπογραφία αρχαία και σημερινή της Σάμου.* Ermoupolis.

Kuhn DCG, 1826, *Medicorum Graecorum Opera quae existant* XII 168-179.

Kyrieleis H, 1981, *Fuhrer durch das Heraion von Samos*, Athens.

Launay L de, 1895, Notes sur Lemnos, *Rev. Archeologique Series 3*, 27, 318-23.

Lawless HT, CJ Corrigan and CB Lee, 1994, Interactions of astringent substances, *Chemical Senses* 19, 141-154.

Larson J, 2007, *Ancient Greek Cults: a guide.* London: Routledge.

Levidis A, 1994, *Πλίνιος ο Πρεσβύτερος, περί της Ελληνικής Ζωγραφικής, 35ο Βιβλίο της Φυσικής Ιστορίας.* Athens: Agra Press.

Liddell HG and R Scott, 1879, *Greek-English Lexicon.* Oxford: OUP.

Mahaney WC and R Krishnamani, 2003, Understanding geophagy in anmals: standard procedures for sampling soils. *J. Chem. Ecology* 29, 1503-23.

Maihows J, 1763, *Voyage en France, en Italie et aux Isles de l'Archipel, ou lettres Ecrites du plusieurs endroits de l'Europe et du Levant en 1750.*

Paris.

Mayor A, 2006, *Greek fire, poison arrows and scorpion bombs: biological and chemical warfare in the ancient world.* Woodstock New York: Overlook.

MacGregor, A.G. (editor), 1994, *Sir Hans Sloane: collector, scientist, antiquary, founding father of the British Museum.* London: British Museum.

McNulty AE, 2000, Industrial Minerals in Antiquity: Melos in the Classical and Roman Periods. Unpublished PhD thesis, University of Glasgow.

Mehta D, 2007, *British national formulary 53.* London: British Medical Association and Royal Pharmaceutical Society.

Mendoni LG and AJ Mazarakis-Ainian (eds.), 1998, *Kea - Kythnos. History and Archaeology.* Athens.

Messineo G, 1993, Efestia (Lemno). Area Sacra: Il Nuovo Hieron (Scavi 1979-81), *Annuario Scuola Archaeologica Atene* LXVI-LXVII, 379-425.

Millard AR, 1999, Geochemistry and the early alum industry. In AM Pollard (ed.) *Geoarchaeology: exploration, environments, resources.* Geological Society Special Publication 165: London, 139-146.

Mottana A, 2006, Nicander on stones and inorganic materials, *Rend. Fis. Acc. Lincei* s. 9, 17, 333-353.

Mourughan K, and MP Suryakanth, 2004, Evaluation of an alum-containing mouthrinse for inhibition of salivary *streptococcus mutans* levels in children—a controlled clinical trial. *J. Indian Soc. Pedod. Prev. Dent.* 22, 100-105.

Munster S, 1556, *Cosmographie Universelle.* Basel.

Norton S, 2006, The Pharmacology of Mithridatum: A 2000-Year-Old Remedy, *Molecular Interventions* 6:2, 60-66.

O'Driscoll M, 1989, Bentonite: overcapacity in need of markets. In G Clarke (ed.) *Industrial clays.* London: Metal Bulletin, 55–71.

Oikonomopoulou A, 2005, Η αλλοτριοφαγία των εγκύων στη λαϊκή ιατρική παράδοση. Επιστημονική προσέγγιση, Iatriko Vima, 98 (May– June 2005, Ιούνιος 2005, 98-102.

Olivieri A, 1935, 1950, *Libri medicinales.* Berlin: Akademie-Verlag.

Paximadas SA, 2002, *Λημνία γή, Το πρώτο παγκοσμίως πρότυπο φαρμακευτικό προϊόν.* Athens: Ellinika Grammata.

Palache C, H Berman and C. Frondel, 1944, *Dana's System of Mineralogy.* New York: John Wiley & Sons Inc.

Papageorgiadou-Banis Ch, 1997, The *Coinage of Kea, ΜΕΛΕΤΗΜΑΤΑ 24.*Athens: National Hellenic Research Foundation.

Pennas C, 1994, To mesioniko frourio Kotsinos tes Lemnou, *Archaiologia* 50, 69-76.

Perna M, 2005, L'alun dans les documents en Lineaire B. In P. Borgard, JP.

Brun and M. Picon (eds), *L'Alun de Meditérranée. Colloque Interna-tional, Naples, Lipari Juin 2003*. Naples, Aix-en-Provence: Centre Jean Bérard, 39-42.

Photos-Jones E, Atkinson, JA, Hall AJ and I Banks 1998, The bloomery mounds of the Scottish Highlands, Part 1: The archaeological back-ground. *J. Historical Metallurgy Soc.* 32, 15-32.

Photos-Jones E, AJ Hall, V Perdikatsis, S Chiotis and E Demou, 2000, In-dustrial minerals exploitation in antiquity in the Aegean: the case of Lemnian Earth, Unpublished SASAA 13 Report for General Secre-tariat of Research and Technology, Ministry of Development, Athens and British Council, Athens.

Photos-Jones E, Cottier, A, Hall AJ and Mendoni LG, 1997, Keian miltos: the well known iron oxides of Antiquity, *Ann. British School at Ath-ens* 92, 359-71.

Photos-Jones E, AJ Hall, JA Atkinson, G Tompsett, A Cottier and GDR Sanders, 1999, The Aghia Kyriaki, Melos survey: Prospecting for the elusive earths in the Roman period in the Aegean, *Ann. British School at Athens* 94, 377-413.

Photos-Jones E and AJ Hall, 2010, *Stypteria phorime* as alunogen in solu-tion: Possible pointer to the gradual cooling of the Melos geothermal system, *Hellenic J. Geosciences* 45, 217-226.

Photos-Jones E and AJ Hall, in press, *Eros Mercator and the Productive Landscape of Melos*. Glasgow: Potingair Press.

Pittinger J, 1975, The mineral products of Melos in antiquity and their iden-tification, *Ann. British School at Athens* 70, 191-197.

Plaitakis A and RC Duvoisin, 1983, Homer's moly identified as *Galanthus nivalis L.*: physiologic antidote to stramonium poisoning, *Clin. Neu-ropharmacology* 6:1, 1–5.

Plimer I and N Petrou, 2000, *Milos: Geologic History*, Athens: Koan.

Psaropoulou B, 1986, *Last potters of the East Aegean.* Nauplion: Pelopon-nese Folklore Foundation.

Reinbacher WR, 2003, *Healing Earths: The Third Leg of Medicine.A His-tory of Minerals in Medicine*, 1st Books Library, Bloomington, Indi-ana.

Rauber-Lüthy C, U Halbsguth, J Kupferschmidt, N König, C Mégevand, K Zihlmann and A Ceschi, 2010, Low-dose exposure to Veratrum al-bum in children causes mild effects - a case series, *Clinical Toxicol-ogy* 48:3, 234–237.

Renfrew AC, 2004, Cognitive Archaeology. In C Renfrew and P Bahn (eds) *Archaeology: The Key Concepts.* London: Routledge, 41-45.

Richardson WD, 1927, *The current significance of the word alum.* Chicago: Commonwealth Press.

Riddle, JM, 1985, *Dioscorides on pharmacy and medicine.* Austin, Texas:

University of Texas.

Robertson AHF and JE Dixon, 1984, Introduction: aspects of the geological evolution of the Eastern Mediterranean. In JE Dixon and AHF Robertson (eds.) *The Geological Evolution of the Eastern Mediterranean*. London: Geological Society, Blackwell Scientific, 1-74.

Robertson RHS, 1986, *Fuller's Earth: A History of Calcium Montmorillonite*. Hythe: Volturna Press.

Rowland ID and Noble Howe T, 1999, *Vitruvius: Ten Books on Architecture*. Cambridge: CUP.

Sealey FLW, 1919, Lemnos, *Annual British School at Athens* 22, 164-5.

Shelford P, 1982, The Geology of Melos. In AC Renfrew and M Wagstaff (eds) *An Island Polity: the Archaeology of Exploitation in Melos*. Cambridge: CUP, 74-81 and Appendix B.

Shipley G, 1987, *A History of Samos 800-188 BC*. Oxford: OUP.

Sigerist HE, 1961, *A History of Medicine II. Early Greek, Hindu and Persian Medicine*. Oxford: OUP.

Simandoni-Bournia E, L Mendoni and TM Panagou, 2009, *Καρθαία. Ελαχύνωτον στέρνον χθονός*. Athens: Greek Ministry of Culture Publications.

Simmons WH and HA Appleton, 2007, *The Handbook of Soap Manufacture*. London.

Singer C, 1927, The Herbal in Antiquity and Its Transmission to Later Ages, *J Hellenic Studies* 47, 1-52.

Singer C, 1948, *The Earliest Chemical Industry: An essay in the historical relations of economics & technology illustrated from the alum trade*. London: The Folio Society.

Smoot TW, 1963, Clay minerals in ceramic industries. *Proc 10th Conference Clays and Clay Minerals*, 309–17.

Stamatakis MG, U Lutat, M Regueiro and JP Calvo, 1996, Milos: The mineral island. *Industrial Minerals*, February, 57- 61.

Stamatakis MG and GS Economou, 1991, A colemanite and ulexite occurrence in Late Miocene saline-alkaline lake of west Samos, Greece, *Economic Geology* 86, 166-172.

Stamatakis MG, JR Hein and AC Magganas, 1989, Geochemistry and diagenesis of Miocence lacustrine siliceous sedimentary and pyroclastic rocks, Mytilini basin, Samos Island, Greece, *Sedimentary Geology* 64, 65-78.

Stamatakis MG, EP Tzritis and N Evelpidou, 2009, The geochemistry of boron-rich groundwater of the Karlovassi Basin, Samos Island, Greece, *Central European J. Geosciences* 1, 207-218.

Stephanides MK, 1898, *Η Ορυκτολογία του Θεοφράστου*. Athens.

Sweet JM, 1935, Sir Hans Sloane: Life and mineral collection, *Natural History Magazine* 5, 145-164.

113

Sweetman SC (ed.), 2007, *Martindale: The Complete Drug Reference.* London: Pharmaceutical Press.

Taj A and R Baquai, 2007, Antimicrobial effects of alum and sulphur on bacteria isolated from mineral and hospital water, *J. Pakistan Infect. Dis.* 16, 10-13.

Theodoropoulos D, 1979, Geological map of Greece, 1:50000, Island of Samos. IGME, Athens.

Thevet A, 1575, *La cosmographie universelle d'André Thevet, Cosmographe du Roy: illustrée de diverses figures des choses plus remarquables vues par l'auteur, & inconus de nos anciens & modernes* II. Paris: Guillaume Chaudière.

Thompson CJS, 1914, Terra Sigillata, a famous medicament of ancient times, *Proceedings of the 17th International Congress of Medicine.* 23, 433-444.

Tourptsoglou-Stephanidou V, 1986, *Taxiodiotika ke Geograhica kemena ya tin neson Lemno (15ᵒ-20ᵒ aeonas)* (Geographic and Travellers accounts about the island of Lemnos (15ᵗʰ-20ᵗʰ centuries). Thessaloniki: University of Salonika, The Polytechnic School.

Tran N, A Mir, D Mallik, A Sinha, S Nayar and TJ Webster, 2010, Bactericidal effect of iron oxide nanoparticles on Staphylococcus aureus, *Int. J. Nanomedicine* 15:5, 277-83.

Von Staden H, 1989, *Herophilus: the art of medicine in early Alexandria: edition, translation and essays.* Cambridge: CUP.

Vukovic Z, A Milutonovic, L Rozc, Z Nedic and D Jovanovic, 2006, The influence of acid treatment on the composition of bentonite, *Clays and Clay Minerals* 54, 697-702.

Williams LB, EH Shelley and RE Ferrell, 2009, Bentonite, bandaids and borborygmi, *Elements* 5, 99-104.

Wilson MJ, 2003, Clay mineralogical and related characteristics of geophagic materials, *J. Chemical Ecology* 29: 7, 1525-1543.

Whitbread IK, 1995, *Greek Transport Amphorae. A Petrological and Archaeological Study. The British School at Athens, Fitch Laboratory Occasional Papers 4.* Athens: The British School at Athens.

Woywodt A and A Kiss, 2002, Geophagia: the history of earth eating, J. *Roy. Soc. Med.* 9, 143-6.

Young S, 2011, *Craving Earths: why do some people love eating dirt?* Columbia: Columbia University Press.

Web sites

ToVima 2010 (http://www.tovima.gr/finance/finance-international-news/article/?aid=382852)

Skaltsa 2001 (http://www.ethnopharmacology.gr/images/stories/ekdiloseis/2001_04/ skaltsa.pdf)

Glossary of geological and geotechnical terms

acid sulphate alteration - a type of hydrothermal alteration that results when sulphur is oxidised to produce sulphuric acid.

albite - a feldspar mineral, $NaAlSi_3O_8$.

alluvial - deposited by flowing water.

alum - the general name for a group of minerals which are soluble aluminum-rich sulphates. Potassium alum (K-alum), $KAl(SO_4)_2.12H_2O$ is the main mineral of the group.

alunite - $KAl_3(SO_4)_2(OH)_6$. It is relatively insoluble.

amorphous - lacking a crystalline structure. Minerals are crystalline.

andesite - a rock formed from a calc-alkali lava and rich in the mineral andesine indicative of a composition that is intermediate between mafic and felsic.

apatite - $Ca_5(PO_4)_3(OH,F,Cl)$ a mineral found in rocks but also a major component of bone.

bedrock - the solid rock that usually underlies soil or sediment.

calcite - $CaCO_3$, a common mineral found in many rock types.

calcareous sandstone - a sandstone that is rich in calcite, usually forming a calcitic cement holding particles of sand together.

calc-alkali - rich in calcium and sodium.

chlorite - a magnesium and iron-rich layered aluminous silicate mineral often found in altered volcanic rocks and in metamorphic rocks such as schists. It is also found in sediments and clays. It has a 14Å interlayer spacing and is not expanding.

cinnabar - HgS, a crimson red mineral well known in antiquity and used as a pigment.

clay - a sediment with very small (<2 microns) particles.

clay mineral - usually taken to mean a layered silicate, rich in silica and alumina but often with additional cations; and may be much larger than 2 microns in size.

clinoptilolite - $(Na,K,Ca)_{2-3}Al_3(Al, Si)_2Si_{13}O_{36}.12H_2O$, a type of zeolite with a complex composition, formed on alteration of volcanic tuffs.

cristobalite - one of the silica-group minerals, SiO_2 typically in fine white crystals.

conglomerate - sedimentary rock rich in large pebbles or boulders.

detrital - sedimented particles, usually deposited from water.

expanding clay - Refers to clay minerals (especially smectites) which have a large capacity to expand with gain, and contract with loss, of water and other molecules which can be held within the layered structure of the clay mineral. Expanding clays are also strongly 'absorbing' and have a large cation exchange capacity as some cations and molecules are exchanged in the interlayer spacing preferentially for others. The ability to absorb moisture, various metallic cations and some organic molecules is probably the main basis of the medical properties of expanding/swelling/absorbing clays.

fault - fracture in rock, often a fracture zone usually with a displacement of rock on either side of the fault.

feldspar - a group name with two main compositional sub-groups, $(K,Na)AlSi_3O_8$ and $(Ca,Na)AlSi_3O_8$.

felsic - an igneous rock which is rich in feldspars and silica so usually rich in sodium, calcium, potassium, aluminium and silicon.

gneiss - a rock formed at the highest grade of regional metamorphism with a banded fabric so that it resembles an interlayered granite and schist.

goethite - $FeOOH$, a common ferric iron mineral, an oxidation product of many iron-bearing minerals.

gypsum - $CaSO_4.2H_2O$, a common mineral that is usually a pointer to evaporitic conditions (evaporation of sulphate-rich seawater) when it is found in sediments.

hematite - An iron oxide, Fe_2O_3, containing iron in the oxidized form, ie ferric iron, $Fe^{...}$, rather than the reduced Fe^{2+} form. It is metallic black, but has a rich red colour when very fine.

hydrothermal - hot water solution.

idiomorphic - with a well-defined shape.

igneous - (or magmatic) rocks formed by cooling of melts.

illite - a 10 Å, clay fraction muscovite-like mineral with a very variable chemical composition. It is non-expanding but may contain layers of expanding smectite clay (a mixed-layer clay). Illite is a common clay component of soils and fine sediments.

intrusive - igneous rocks formed by injection of molten rocks, often in form of a vertical (dyke) or horizontal (sill) sheet.

iron oxyhydroxide - general name for hydrated iron minerals that contain hydroxyl (-OH) groups and may contain water molecules (H_2O) and have a variable iron valency but often Fe^{3+}. They may be well or poorly crystallized. They have a yellow brown to reddish-brown colour and are often called 'limonite'. Goethite is an example. Iron rust is essentially iron oxyhydroxide.

iron sulphides - the common iron sulphide mineral in rocks is pyrite FeS_2 but there are others. All are very susceptible to oxidation on weathering to produce iron oxyhydroxides and sulphate.

kaolin - a 7 Å clay group; kaolinite is $Al_2Si_2O_5(OH)_4$.

lime - CaO. Very rare as a mineral since very unstable but formed readily on heating of calcite, $CaCO_3$, the main constituent of limestone.

limonite - see iron oxyhydroxides.

mafic - an igneous rock rich in magnesium and iron and usually dark coloured.

magmatic - (or igneous) formed from a melt, e.g. lava.

magnesite -the mineral magnesium carbonate, $MgCO_3$ which is white.

marble - strictly a metamorphosed limestone consisting mainly of calcite.

marl - fine sedimentary rock which is rich in clay minerals and calcite.

metamorphism - geological process that leads to change in a rock usually due to high temperature and pressure.

mica - usually a muscovite-like mineral, $KAl_2(Si_3Al)O_{10}(OH)_2$ with 10Å basal spacing.

mineral - A mineral can be defined as: a naturally occurring chemical compound with a definite chemical composition and atomic structure. Minerals have names approved by an International Association and can usually be identified from their appearance and properties. Minerals were often named after localities and the same mineral could have been given different names. These anomalies have gradually been removed but there are still 'obsolete' mineralogical names and terms in use. Note that a 'rock' is usually defined as consisting of one or more minerals.

mineralisation - the process, usually geothermal, of the generation of new minerals, some of which are usually of economic value.

montmorillonite - a name for a group of expanding clays with a basal spacing of about 15Å at normal humidity, $(Na,Ca)_{0.3}(Al,Mg)_2Si_4O_{10}(OH)_2.nH_2O$. Montmorillonite can be calcium or sodium-rich. Fine sediments or rocks which are rich in montmorillonite usually result from the alteration of igneous rocks such as volcanic ashes and are known as bentonite or fuller's earth.

mordenite - $(Na_2,K_2,Ca)Al_2Si_{10}O_{24}.7H_2O$, a type of zeolite which is quite common in altered volcanic rocks.

phenocryst - large crystal set in a finer-grained matrix in an igneous rock.

pozzolana - volcanic ash which reacts with water and lime to form a cement in concrete giving the concrete the ability to set under water.

pyroclastic rocks - rocks rich in fragments of volcanic origin, including tuff.

quartz - SiO_2 This is the commonest form of silica and, because of its hardness and chemical resistance, is usually a major constituent of sediments (from clays to conglomerates). It is also present in many other rock types.

quartz sandstone - a sandstone with detrital particles of quartz.

sandstone - sedimentary rock with sand-size particles, usually of quartz but can be of any rock material.

saponite - a smectite mineral formed on hydrothermal alteration of mafic igneous rocks.

schist—rock with schistose metamorphic fabric resulting from deformation.

secondary mineral - a mineral usually formed as a result of low temperature hydration of an earlier 'primary' mineral.

SEM - scanning electron microscopy - a technique for high magnification that is evolving rapidly and ideal for observing and characterising chemically very small fragments of minerals.

serpentinite - a metamorphic rock rich in iron and magnesium, and formed by hydration of an ultramafic igneous rock.

silicified - converted to being rich in silica, usually as the mineral, quartz.

smectite - The group name favoured by the International Mineralogical Association for the expanding clays.

tectonism - deformation of rocks resulting in folds and faults.

thrust - a low-angle fault.

tuff - volcanic ash.

unconformity - a discontinuity in sedimentation with underlying older sedimentary rocks at an angle due to tectonsim and with overlying younger sediments or sedimentary rocks. The unconformity is usually an essentially horizontal plane that results from erosion before the overlying sediments have been deposited.

XRD - X-ray diffraction spectrometry - a simple technique for identifying minerals based on fingerprinting the atomic structure.

zeolite - a group of aluminosilicate minerals that have a porous, open-framework structure that results in them having absorbent and catalytic properties.

INDEX of names and place names

Aghia Hypate (*Ayia Ypate, Hagiapate, Aghios Ypatios*)...48,95;
Aghia Kyriaki...85,86,87,88;
Apelles ...71,72;
Argentiera....68;
Aristophanes *Clouds*...11;
Aristophanes *Lysistrata*...23,25;
Aristophanes...9,11,23,25,67;
Belon ... 9,15,22,23,27,30,31,33,34,35,37,38,40,44,90,93,96,98,99,104;
Celsus ... 11,68;
Cleigenis... 66,67;
Covel...13,93,94,95,96;
De Launay...25,44,45,91,96105;
Dioscorides...3,6,8,10,17,18,28,39,57,58,64,65,68,70,78,83,88,89,99,102;
Euboea..... 6,8,64,65;
Galen...3,4,5,6,10,11,12,17,18,21,25,28,29,30,33,35,37,40,41,42,43,44,47,
55,58,68,76,89,91,92,94,95,96,97,98,99,101,102,104;
Lemnian Earth...
3,4,5,6,7,12,13,14,19,20,21,22,23,28,29,30,31,32,33,34,35,36,37,40,43,44,
45,46,49,5355,56,68,70,90,91,92,93,95,96,97,98,99,100,101,102,104,105;
Hephaistias...3,4,22,23,27,32,33,40,41,42,43,44,45,46,47,48,52,99;
Hephaistos...3,22,23,24,25,27,29,45,47,51,103;
Herodotus...23,26,31,57;
Hesiod [*Theogony*] ... 23,24;
Hippocrates...10,12,81;
Homer...9,10,11,12,22,26,64,86;
Ioulis...73,74;
Kalamos...87,88;
Kassandra...88;
Kastro Vouni...23,27,33,35,41,44,45,46,47,48;
Kea...6,8,28,72,73,74,75,76,77;
Kimolos (or *Cimolos*)...6,8,68,69,70;
Knidos ... 88;
Kotsinas (or *Kotzinos*)...32,33,34,35,37,38,39,40,43,48,93;
Kyzicos ... 88;
Lelantine Plain ... 32,65;
Lemnos...2,3,4,5,6,7,8,13,22,23,24,25,26,27,29,30,31,32,33,35,44,45,47,50,
51,52,90,93,99,103,104;
Loulos 82;
Melos ... 6,8,20,68,69,70,72,78,79,80,81,82,83,84,85,86,87,88,89,98;
Mons Vulcani... 22,27,44;

Mosychlos ... 22,24,27,44;
Mycenaean ...73,84,103;
Odysseus... 9,10,26,86;
Odyssey... 9,10,22,23,86;
Orkos ...74,75,77;
Paleochori ... 86;
Paracelscus... 20;
Pausanias ... 24;
Pelasgians ... 26,103;
Philoctetes... 3,22,23,25,26,27,29,103;
Philostratus...29,103;
Phtheleidia spring (related to the Lemnian
Earth)...32,33,36,37,38,39,40,49,95,104;
Pliny on alum...84;
Pliny on ambelitis... 88;
Pliny on Eretrian Earth... 64;
Pliny on labyrinths... 45;
Pliny on Melian Earth...81;
Pliny on *Pnigitis* Earth 89;
Pliny on sulphur... 86;
Pliny on Tymphaic gypsum... 89;
Pliny...11,17,18,19,21,29,45,55,56,58,64,68,70,71,72,81,84,85,86,88,89,99,
101;
Plutarch...81;
Pyrgi... 70;
Samos ... 3,6,8,57,58,59,60,61,62;
Sinopic *miltos* ...72;
Sloane [Sir Hans]...21;
Sophocles on *Philoctetes*...3,22,23,25,26,27,29,103;
Sophocles... 11,23,25,26,29;
Theophrastus ...10,17,18,19,28,55,57,59,60,64,68,72,73,78,88,89,99,105;
    on *ambelitis*...188;
    on Eretrian Earth...17;
    on Kimolian Earth...68;
    on Melian Earth...78;
    on Samos...57;
    on Silenusian Earth....89;
    on Tymphaic gypsum...89;
Trypospilies...74,76,77;
Tymphaia...89;
Vitruvius...30,81;
Vulcan (in Italy) (and see Mons Vulcani, Lemnos)...24;

GENERAL INDEX

absorbents...70;
active ingredient...57,91,98,101,102,105;
alchemy...101;
allotriophagia...12,13;
altered white rock...78,83;
alum:
    [general]...6,8,17,18,53,55,56,57,62,83,84,85,86,90,91,96,
    97,98,99,100,102,103,104;
    harvesting...86;
    history of alum...84
    Linear B...84;
    from mines /caves ...85;
aluminium sulphate...55,56,84,85,98,100;
alunite...53,54,79,83,84,85,98,100,102;
alunogen...55,86,88;
Alzheimer's disease...56
Ambelitis...6,8,88;
   pharmakitis...88;
antibacterial...7,14,56,57,63;
antibiotics...8,101;
antidote...4,6,12,28,29,102;
antiseptic...8,62,63;
Apelles' palette...71,72;
archaeological evidence for Lemnian Earth...32,40;
archaeological identity...6;
archaeological record...7;
archaeological survey...74;
Armenian Bole...30;
aster...8,17,58,60;
astringency....15,55,56,100,102,104;
ayiasma (sacred water)...22,27,34,35,101;
ayiochoma (sacred Lemnian Earth)...31,34,53,101;
back-filled 'pit'...52;
bacteria...7,14,27,56,57,63,103,105;
bactericide...57,102;
bacteriostasis...14;
belief...13,30,101,105;
bentonite...16,59,60,61,62,68,69,70,71,78;
biochemical research [more on aluminium needed]...56;
borate...42,60,62,63,105;
boron...59,60,62,105;

castle at Kotsinas...32,33,34,38,101;
cation exchange of clays...14;
cave...27,39,74,75,85;
chemical analysis...19,62,103,105;
Chian Earth...8,70,71;
china clay (kaolin) in Melian Earth...16,82;
Chios:
    volcanics...6,71;
Church [the]...6,101;
cinnabar...29, 99;
clay...5,6,7,8,12,13,14,15,16,17,20,21,25,31,32,35,36,40,42,43,46,51,52,53,
54,56,57,59,60,62,63,64,65,67,68,69,70,82,90,91,95,96,97,99,100,102,103,
104,105;
cleaning cloth...8,68;
Cleigenis' Soap:
    [general]...66;
    valanefs...67;
colemanite...62,63;
colyrium, an eye salve...58;
cosmetics...6,68;
creta...6,8,64,68;
curative properties...30,91;
current research into fine iron oxides...74;
deodorant [natural, alum]...57;
dye...11,55,56,68,84,88;
Earths: general]...6,7,8,9,10,11,12,13,15,1718,19,20,2132,36,46,54,
55,56,69,83,84,88,90,95,101;
    as composite materials...15,20;
    on eating earth...12,13;
    function of earths...15,55,56;
    future investigation....20;
    formulae..19;
efflorescences...59,85;
Epsom salts...83,85;
Eretrian Earth (*terra eretria*) *creta eretria* (κρητις):
    [general]...8,17,32,58,64,78,89;
    properties...8,17,89;
Euboea:
    marble...65;
excavations [at Hephaestias]...27,41,42;
expanding clay...16,46,51,54,97;
experimental work [on Melian alum]...86;
exploitation...20,64,87;

experimental work [on Melian alum]....86;
exploitation....20,74,87;
extraction...5,6,11,20,23,30,30,32,35,36,37,38,45,59,63,84,92,93,95,101,
102,104;
eye-salve...58;
fine-grained hematite, ferric oxide...73,77;
fuller's earth...16,60,68,69;
fulling...8,86;
geophagia...2,13,14,105;
geothermal...7,25,78,79,80,81,98;
geotragia...12;
geyser...79;
grades...6,30,35,95,102,104;
gypsum [in efflorescences]...85;
haemostatic [alum]...55;
Hematite....28,73,76,77,91,96,99,100,104;
herb-based medicines...9
hieron at Hephaestias...41,42,43,45;
hot springs...68,78,79,81;
hot water...79,81,97;
hydrothermal alteration ... 40,47,50,51,54,76,97,98,99,103;
hydrothermal solution...54,76,77,98;
illite...16,53,91,100;
industrial heritage on Melos...80
industrial minerals of antiquity...6;
iron content of Lemnian Earth...91;
iron deposits of Kea...74,76;
iron impurity in alum...56;
iron oxide...28,51,73,74,75,76,77,90,91,100;
kaolin(ite) (China clay)...14,15,16,46,51,54,79,82,83,85,96,97,100,104;
Kastro Vouni:
    underground chamber... 45;
Kea
    see *miltos*
    archaeological survey on Kea...74;
    city states of Kea...73,74;
    limonite…76,77;
    mineralization...76;
    volcanics...6,75;
Kimolian Earth...8,17,66,67,68,69,70;
Kimolos:
    pozzolana...89;
    silver mineralisation (lack of)...68;

volcanic...6,68,70;
Lapis Samius [Samian Stone]...58;
Lemnia rubrica [for Lemnian Earth]...29;
Lemnian bole (βώλου της Λημνίας) ...29;
Lemnian crime...23,26,103;
Lemnian Earth:
    medicinal...3,8,17,20,21,28,30,32,90,95,96,99,100,103,104,105;
    Λημνία γή in Dioscorides...3,6,8,17,28,99,102;
    colour...4,5,17,28,30,31,35,43,47,53,54,91,93,95,97,98,99,100;
    commercial aspects of...30;
    composition...21,28,90,96,98,100,104;
    extraction...5,6,23,30,32,33,35,36,37,38,45,92,93,95,101,102,104;
    future research...35,43;
    healing properties...7,22,23,31,100,101;
    how and why the Earths worked...21,99,102;
    processing...6,20,43,93,95,102;
    pottery making...31,34,35,43;
    remedy for bites and stings...28;
    day of the extraction...592;
    documentary evidence...32,96,97,99;
    use for dysentery...29,102;
    holy water [agiasma]...34,101;
    mineralogical study...90;
    in modern pharmacology...102;
    montmorillonite...53,54,57,91,96,97,99,100,103,104;
    pagan ritual... 6,101;
    pellet...4,5,6,91,93;
    pharmakides...11,101;
    pit...36,37,53,91,92,93,94,95,96,99,100,102,103,104;
    placebo...91;
    recipe...57,96;
    as plague remedy... 4,30;
    pottery kilns...35;
    poultice...91;
    priestess ... 5,12,44,47,92,95;
    procession...5,47,91;
    remedy for snake bites...6,11;
    research priority...102;
    ritual...5,6,31,33,90,92,99,100,102,104;
    sacred earth...31,93,101;
    sigillata...29,90,93,99;
    smectitic clay...14,46,100,103;

soluble alum [in spring water]...98,102,103;
sphragides...4;
sphragidite (an aluminosilicate of sodium) 90,91;
sphragis ...28,29,90,92;
swelling [re Lemnian Earth] ... 91,103;
terra Lemnia...22,29,44,99;
terra rubricata [in Pliny *Nat. Hist.*]...29,99;
terra sigi(l)lata...20,29,90,93,99;
therapeutic properties...30,31;
travellers...30,31,33,92,96,99;
varieties of Lemnian Earth...30,31,35,54,93,96,98;
washing...48,92,95,96,97,101,102,104;
weight of troches of Lemnian Earth...30,31;
facts...28;
records of geological, environmental and anthropogenic events...103;
related myths...22;
route [of Galen] ...37,38,40,41,47;
taste of Lemnian Earth... 100;
where to find it...32;
Lemnian fire...23,25;
Lemnian *miltos* (μίλτος)...4,28,29,99;
Lemnian *sphragis* (σφραγίς Λημνία)...28,29,92;
Lemnos:
 [general]...2,3,4,5,6,7,8,13,22,23,24,25,26,27,29,30,31,32,33,35,44,45,
47,50,51,52,90,93,99,103,104;
 Volcanic [re Lemnos]...3,6,10,22,25,33,34,39,47,50,53,54,59,90,96,97,
98,102,103
Lithos Samios (Stone of Samos)...58;
lye...66,67;
medical geology...7;
medical websites, ('fringe')...62;
medicinal...3,7,8,10,11,13,15,17,18,20,21,28,30,32,55,56,58,62,64,74,90,
95,96,99,100,103,104,105;
Melian *alumen* [nature of]... 84;
Melian Earth
 [general]...8,17,57,72,78,79,81,82,83,85,98;
 Loulos...82;
 medicine, grey Melian Earth...81;
 polishing powder...78;
 workings of Melian Earth at Loulos...82;
Melos:
 see also Melian Earth, alum and sulphur;
 alum...6,8,20,68,69,70,78,79,80,81,82,83,84,85,86,87,88,89,98;

bentonite (Kimolian Earth)...68,69,70;
soil...85,86;
solfatara...78,85,87,88;
sulphur...8,79,84,85,86,87,88,98;
volcanic...6,78,79,80,81,84,86;
metamorphic rocks...80;
millowite...83;
miltos:
    [general]...4,6,8,17,18,28,29,72,73,74,76,77,99;
    mentioned by Nicander...28;
    artificial...73;
    export from Kea...73;
    Lemnian miltos....4,28,29,99;
    Lemnian Earth...15,38;
    mentioned in The *Herbal* of Dioscorides... 8;
    uses...73;
    astringent *(styptike)* Kean *miltos*...74;
    goethite in relation to Kean *miltos*...76,77;
    limestone caves related to Kean *miltos*...75;
    manganese in Kean *miltos*...77;
    marble-rich areas around Kean *miltos*...74,75,76;
    mine galleries...75;
    styptike (astringent*)* Kean *miltos*...74;
    Tetrabiblon...74;
    the colour red: *Miltos* of Kea ...73;
    underground workings...74,76;
    mineral enrichment as ritual...90
mineral-based medicines...101;
minor earths...88;
moly...10;
montmorillonite...14,16,46,51,53,54,57,68,69,70,91,96,97,99,100,103,
104,105;
mordant ... 6,7,8,17,55,84;
myth...22,23,24,25,27,29,44,45,46,51,101,103,104,105;
nano-particle level...14;
paint...16,18,19,57,71,72,73,77,78,81,83,89;
*pharmacognos*y...10;
pharmaka...9,10,11,12,101;
pharmakopoles... 11;
pharmakotrives... 11,19;
pharmasso... 11;
Pnigitis Earth or *Terra Pnigitis*...6,8,89;
poisons...4,11,12,28,29;

potter, Nikolaos Tsoukalas.....34;
pottery workshop/kiln in Kotsinas....31,34,35;
poultice....12,16,74,91;
processing [post-extraction]...6,20,21,43,85,93,95,102;
procession...5,47,91;
purity [re pomegranate juice]...56;
pyroclastic...33,50,53,60,70,98;
raw material...7,21,28,104;
red [ochreous matrix, re altered rock] ...54;
ritual...5,6,31,33,42,43,90,92,99,100,101,102,103,104;
route 33,37,38,39,40,41,47,56,88;
Samian Earth:
    [general]...8,17,21,32,57,58,59,60,62,70,78,105;
    weight [density] of Samian Earth...57;
    properties ... 8,17,21,57,59,62;
    use for epilepsy...58;
Samian Stone *[Lapis Samius]* ... 58;
workings [of Samian Earth] ... 57,60;
Samos
Samos [general]...8,57,58,59,60,61,62;
    limestones...59;
    marble..59;
    volcanic... 6,59,60;
    walled terraces ...60;
sealed earth [Lemnian Earth] ... 31,35,38;
seals [as seen by Belon and illustrated in his book] ... 5,31,92;
SEM [Melian alum] ... 86,87;
    [Melian sulphur] ... 87,88;
    [Samian borate] ... 60,62,63,105;
semandrida ge... 31;
Silenusian Earth or *Terra Selinusiae*.... 89;
smectite... 14,16;
snails [land snails] ... 52;
snake bites... 4,5,6,29;
soap...58,60,66,67,69;
special 'earths' ... 46;
spring...3,32,33,34,35,36,37,38,39,40,47,48,49,53,54,55,57,68,78,79,81,92,
93,94,95,96,97,98,99,100,102,103,104;
stypteria [alum] ...84;
styptic [alum] ... 10,55,56,68;
sulphur disinfectant, sulphur...86;
sulphur ...6,8,17,18,51,54,67,79,84,85,86,87,88,98;
    [collection at Kalamos, Melos]... 87;

[mentioned in the Herbal of Dioscorides]...6,8,18;
   grains [from a Melian fumaroles views on SEM]....87;
      medicine [sulphur, Melos].... 86;
Melian solfataras [re sulphur, Melos]...78,79,85,87,88;
 mineralisation [re sulphur, Melos]...87;
sulphurous Melian fumarole ...79,85,88;
symptom... 20,27,28;
tannic acids [re astringency] ... 56;
taste [general]...10,100;
   [re astringency] ... 55,56;
terra rossa battuta [compressed red earth, re Hephaistias] ... 42,43;
tetrachromia ... 72;
textiles ...55,84;
therapeutic uses [of sulphur, Melos] ...86;
therapeutic...7,17,30,31,86;
toxins...12,14;
travellers...30,31,33,92,96,99;
uses [of alum] ...55;
uses [of Earths]...4,55,59,62,64,68,70,73,86,99;
varieties of alum...84;
volcanic rocks [altered]...16,40,50,51,53,54,60,70,71,78,79,80,82,83,97, 98,102;
washing materials [Cleigenis' soap]... 66;
   powders [washing]...66,101;
waste...21,60,85,86;
water snake... 22,26;
white [altered rock] ...54,60,70,78,79,81,82,83,84,85,97,98;
   [Chian Earth] ...8,70,71;
   [efflorescence, Melian alum]...85;
   [Eretrian Earth] ... 8,17,32,58,64,78,89;
   [Melian Earth]...8,17,57,72,78,79,81,82,83,85,98;
   pigment...6,7,8,15,16,17,19,28,30,72,74,76,77,78,81,83,101,105;
workings [of Samian Earth] ... 57,60;
XRD ... 15,35,46,54,62,77,96,97;